START

HERE

Beginning with the Basics of

Spirit-Filled Faith

JOSHUA SARGENT

Start Here

Printed in the United States of America

First Printing, 2011

ISBN-10: 0-615-57458-0
ISBN-13: 978-0-615-57458-5

www.pastorjosh.com

START HERE TABLE OF CONTENTS

Introduction   5

Chapter 1 - Developing a Life of Devotion   9

Chapter 2 – The Basics of Prayer   23

THE 20/20 Challenge   37

Chapter 3 - Understanding Your Salvation   38

Chapter 4 - Receiving the Holy Spirit   53

Chapter 5 – Accepting the Great Commission   69

and Great Commandment

Chapter 6 – Starting to Serve   80

Chapter 7 – Stewardship   93

Conclusion   105

START HERE INTRODUCTION

Did you know there are over two billion people in the world who profess to be Christians? Many millions more commit their lives to Christ every year. Here's the problem: most are not taught the Basics of Spirit-Filled Christianity. When I say the "Basics", I mean how to pray, how to study the Bible, understanding your salvation, understanding the Holy Spirit, the Great Commission, serving, and giving.

I grew up in church but was never taught the Basics of Spirit-Filled Christianity until I was a teenager. My Pastor, James Wells, then taught me what the Bible says about our salvation, how to pray, how to study, and why I should serve. This insight made a huge difference in my life. It helped me become a more stable Christian. Before he taught me the basics, I could not pray for more than five minutes. I felt uncomfortable praying in public. I struggled to understand the Bible. I didn't want to be a witness. Can you relate?

Many professing Christians struggle in their walk with God or quit serving God. Why? I believe it is because they were never given the solid foundation of learning the basics. They committed their lives to Christ, but no one ever explained what to do next. How can we expect someone to complete the race if they never learned how to start? This book will help you grow as a believer, strengthen your walk with God, and encourage you to fulfill God's will for your life.

This book is not a hard read. It is not a hard to understand book on theology, but rather is a simple book on the Basics of Spirit-Filled Christianity. If you were never taught how to pray, how to study the Bible, about the Holy Spirit, loving other people, serving, or tithing, this book is for you. If you are a new Christian, this book is for you. If you are struggling with your walk, this book is for you. In this book, we assume that you have given your heart to Christ, been baptized in water, and are committed to a Bible believing church.

When legendary Green Bay Packers football coach, Vince Lombardi took over the struggling Green Bay Packers in 1958, he was asked, "What are you going to change to turn this team around after a string of failures and losing seasons?"

Coach Lombardi responded: "I am not going to change anything. We will use the same players, the same plays and the same training system. But we will

concentrate on becoming "brilliant at the basics." In nine

seasons, his Green Bay Packers won five NFL

Championships and two Super Bowls.[i]

My challenge to you is to start here and "become

brilliant" at the Basics of Spirit-Filled Faith.

START HERE
BEGINNING WITH THE BASICS OF SPIRIT-FILLED FAITH

CHAPTER 1 - DEVELOPING A LIFE OF DEVOTION

"The Bible is worth all other books which have ever been printed."

Patrick Henry

Have you ever tried to put together something for your kids and did not use the instructions? One year my children received a train set for Christmas from one of their grandparents. You know us men; we see reading the instructions as a sign of weakness. Instead of reading the instructions, I looked at the picture on the box and began assembling over one hundred odd shaped pieces. I did the best I could, but the problem was my train set did not look like the train set on the box and I had fourteen pieces left over!

What did I do? I had to take it all apart and start over but this time I read the directions. It would have saved me time if I had started with the directions in the first place. Let me encourage you to always start with the Word of God. Joshua 1:8 says, "Keep this Book of the Law always on your lips; meditate on it day and night, so that you may be careful to do everything written in it. Then you will be prosperous and successful." (NIV) If you start with the directions, life will be so much easier.

God does not want us to just have a devotional life that is something we have to do every morning or evening out of habit. He wants us to have a relationship with Him where we devote our whole life to Him and His Word. Just participating in a Bible study, belonging to a small group, or reading a book like this one will not make you a disciple.

The Bible says in John 8:31, "If you abide in My Word, you are My disciples indeed." (NIV) Small groups, courses, and books will help you continue in the Word. Studying, meditating on, and obeying the Word of God are the only things that will make you a disciple and nothing else.

We live in a microwave world, where we want it now, but that does not work in the Kingdom of God. The word "disciple" is derived from the word "discipline" and you cannot become a disciple without being disciplined in your walk with God. If you have been a Christian for very long at all, there have been times when you needed to read and study but you were too tired or too busy. Just as an athlete disciplines himself by doing his or her exercises, we must become disciplined in our devotion as people of God.

Many people have a problem reading the Bible because they do not value it as the inspired Word of God. Many people just read the Bible as another book, a novel, or fable. But it is the Holy Word of God to His people. Second Timothy 3:16-17 says, "All Scripture is inspired by God and is useful to teach us what is true and to make us realize what is wrong in our lives. It corrects us when we are wrong and teaches us to do what is right. God uses it to prepare and equip His people to do every good work."

Did you catch that? It said, "ALL scripture is INSPIRED by God!" "Inspired" basically means "God breathed." Since God breathed the Word of God doesn't that change the way you see the Bible? Every scripture and every word is breathed by God!

The Bible also states, in Hebrews 4:12, "For the Word of God is alive and powerful. It is sharper than the sharpest two-edged sword, cutting between soul and spirit, between joint and marrow. It exposes our innermost thoughts and desires." His Word is not a boring book but is life giving and powerful.

You might ask, "Ok, the Bible is the Word of God, but how did we end up with it?" Second Peter 1:21 says, we must "realize that no prophecy in scripture ever came from the prophet's own understanding, or from human initiative. No, those prophets were moved by the Holy Spirit, and they spoke from God." God used people just like us and spoke through them. He did not take over the writers of the Bible as if they were robots, but He inspired them and spoke through them with the Holy Spirit.

Since the Word of God is inspired by God, then we can say three things:

1. **The Bible is true.**

2. **The Bible never fails.**

3. **The Bible is the final authority.**

You might ask, "What about some of the scriptures that are a little bit different in the Gospels?" I explained this one day in one of our services by taking out an article in the newspaper and reading it. Then I asked each person to tell me what stuck out in their mind about the article. Believe it or not, every person remembered a different part of it. They each saw the story from a different perspective.

I believe the same thing happened after the resurrection of Christ. Each disciple reported a different aspect, a different point of view of what happened. They were focusing on the major points. I then asked everyone, "did what each remembered about the article distort the message?" They all uniformly replied "no." The same is true with the accounts in the gospels, there may be a few minor details that are different but the main message is still the same.

The Word of God is the truth. The Bible says in Second Timothy 3:7, that in the last days, people will be, "always learning but never able to come to the knowledge of the truth." There are more Christian books, Christian movies, music, and churches today, but less people are coming to know the truth. Many have not learned to read the Bible for themselves. We must learn to feed ourselves the Word. God wants us to get into the Word and discover the truths.

Make a commitment to God today to begin a life of devotion and a relationship with Him through His Word. We must understand our Christian life is like a race. We must change our thinking about running that race. We've been taught that the race is a grueling marathon, where we can picture ourselves crawling across the finish line because of dehydration. I believe that is why Christians have dropped out of the race! They see themselves in an exhausting race that has no end. They see no rest or help in sight.

In this day, most of our lives relate more to a sprint from the time we wake up to the time we come home from work. We have to get the kids off to school. We have to go to work, drive in traffic, go to meetings, go to appointments, return calls, answer emails, return home, fix dinner, and help clean house. When we sprint all day, we get to go home and enjoy our family, rest, and recover for the next race.

Paul calls our race a sprint. First Corinthians 9:24-26 says "Don't you realize that in a race everyone runs, but only one person gets the prize? So run to win! All athletes are disciplined in their training. They do it to win a prize that will fade away, but we do it for an eternal prize. So I run with purpose in every step."

The Greek word for race was "stadion"; which is defined as "a space or distance of about six hundred feet." Courses of this description were found in most of the larger Greek cities. The same race today would be 600 Greek feet which is one-tenth of a mile today. I believe you can make it one-tenth of mile today! Even if you are in pain you should be able to go one-tenth of a mile. Your daily sprint of one-tenth of a mile involves work, taking care of your business, taking care of your home, family, and being a witness for Christ.

If we are in a daily sprint, we will have to change our habits and spiritual disciplines. If we have a race tomorrow, we cannot fill up on the wrong foods. We have to have fuel physically and spiritually. We get our strength for the race through our devotional time, prayer time, worship time, and rest. We need to start reading our Bible for strength for the race not just to check off our Bible reading plan. We need to pray for God to help us and give us answers for the problems we may experience while in the race. If we are running a daily race, we are going to have to rest at night and take a day of rest, called a "Sabbath" during the week.

If we are so busy with our life that we do not have time for prayer, the Word, worship at church, or rest, we are TOO BUSY! We are striving for the wrong things and running the wrong race. Run the race that is in front of you today, and do not worry about tomorrow's race. Don't worry what others are doing, run your race! We cannot run other people's races. Run your race one day at a time and one step at a time. God is with you all the way! Lace

up your shoes and get in your race. Ready, Set, Go! See

you at the finish line!

Start Here Action Step

Spend at least 20 minutes in God's Word every day.

Read one chapter of Proverbs every day, corresponding to

the date. (For Example: On the first day of the month, read

the first chapter of Proverbs, on the second day, the

second chapter and so on.) Begin reading in the New

Testament, preferably in John, because it covers the

basics. Then start in Matthew and read through the New

Testament.

Start Here Scriptures

Psalm 119:11

Joshua 1:8

John 17:7

Hebrews 4:12

Start Here Memorizing

2 Timothy 3:16 – "All Scripture is given by inspiration of God, and is profitable for doctrine, for reproof, for correction, for instruction in righteousness." (NKJV)

Start Here Discussion Starters

1. What are some benefits of studying the Word of God?

2. What happens when we don't study the Bible?

START HERE: BEGINNING WITH THE BASICS OF SPIRIT-FILLED FAITH

CHAPTER 2 – THE BASICS OF PRAYER

"The most important thing a born again Christian can do is to pray."

Chuck Smith

In 1999, my two-year-old son, Stephen, started having seizures. Seizures are one of the scariest things that could happen to any child.   At the time, Stephen was our only child, and we loved him dearly. After several seizures and many tests, the doctor said the only solution was for Stephen to be put on special medication. The medication may prevent future seizures, but it would also cause his development to be slow for the rest of his life. The doctor said he would give us one day to decide on his recommendation. My wife and I were devastated.

I went home that night to get clothes for us so we could stay in the hospital with Stephen. I remember walking into our apartment and falling on my face before God. I cried out to God and prayed with more passion and urgency than ever before. I cannot remember what I said, but I remember the words were not very eloquent.

I was seriously praying. I was praying from my heart and not my head. The words that I uttered were not fancy but they were full of passion! I loved my son dearly and the prayer I prayed that night, not only changed his life, but also my life.

After much prayer and godly counsel, my wife, Beth, and I decided Stephen did not need the medication prescribed to him by his doctor. The doctor thought we were foolish but we had faith in God. Today, Stephen is a strong and bright young man and hasn't had a seizure since, and we give all the glory to God! God answered our prayers.

Stephen's episode taught me a valuable principle on prayer: the principle of fervency or passion. We need to pray every day with urgency because everything depends on God. Our prayers should reflect the notion that if God does not provide, we're in trouble; and if He doesn't heal, we are going to have to live a life of pain.

Thomas Brooks once said, "As a painted man is no man, and as a painted fire is no fire, so a cold prayer is no prayer." How did you pray for your child when he or she got a high fever in the middle of the night? You would not pray some religious sounding prayer, rather you prayed with passion. You prayed as if your child's life depended upon it! The Bible proclaims that "the earnest prayer of a righteous person has great power and produces wonderful results!" (James 5:16)

We need to understand that prayer must become a part of our lifestyle. We cannot fully understand prayer by just reading a book. Prayer cannot be taught by a simple formula. If that were the case, more people would do it.

We can read what the scriptures say about prayer or read books on it, but prayer is only truly learned by praying. It is just like riding a bicycle: the more we ride, the more comfortable we become riding the bicycle. We get to the point where we do not even have to think about it, but it becomes a part of our life.

Prayer is about having a relationship with God.

As with any relationship, communication is vital. If you do not spend time with your spouse or family, you will not have a very good relationship with them. The same is true with our relationship with God. Many people just use God when they need something, but God wants us, as His children, to communicate with Him every day.

Exodus 33:11 states, "the Lord would speak to Moses face to face, as one speaks to a friend." Not only does God want us to pray to Him, but He wants to speak to us. Prayer must be a dialogue. Most people will come in and tell God their problems and not allow Him to speak to them about the answers. Jeremiah 33:3 says, "Ask me and

I will tell you remarkable secrets you do not know about things to come." We must continually strive to maintain our relationship with the Father.

Prayer is not about how long, how loud, or how fast you pray.

Many people are misled by believing that we have to pray for so long or a certain way before God will hear our prayers. They end up spending more time watching the clock and trying to live up to other people's standards. But you must remember prayer is about a relationship! God looks at the heart of our prayers. I might not have a complete uninterrupted hour every day to spend talking to my wife. The time that I do have I must communicate my love for her and share about our needs and important issues.

When Jesus taught the disciples to pray, He gave them an example to follow. Matthew 6: 9-13 says, "This, then, is how you should pray: 'Our Father in heaven, hallowed be your name, your kingdom come, your will be done, on earth as it is in heaven. Give us today our daily bread. And forgive us our debts, as we also have forgiven our debtors. And lead us not into temptation, but deliver us from the evil one." (NIV)

Jesus taught the disciples to pray for six specific things:

1. God's kingdom and reign to come

2. God's will to be done

3. For God to provide for them

4. For God to forgive them of their sins

5. For God to keep them from temptation

6. For God to deliver them from the evil one

When you pray, be specific about your needs, those you are praying for, and your requests. When you pray you will realize the situations in your life are beyond your control.

The Key to Prayer is Your Attitude.

Intimacy with God is based upon your humility and transparency. James 4:6 says, "God opposes the proud but favors the humble." Jesus illustrates this principle in Luke 18. The Pharisee prayed and thanked God that he was not like the Publican. He fasted twice a week and gave tithes of all that he possessed. He was proud and it kept him from receiving from God!

Pride will hinder your prayer life and keep you from getting your prayers answered. The Publican was humble and when he prayed he would not even look to Heaven. He then asked God for mercy because he was a sinner. What do you imagine he received? He received mercy!

The Pharisee exalted himself and the Publican exalted God. God already knows all of the problems that you face and all the needs that you have. But humility in prayer involves you being honest with yourself and asking God for help. When we are weak, He is strong! Prayer is hard, but living without it is harder. All the resources of heaven are available to you, if you ask. Make time everyday for prayer to God.

My Story

Are you struggling to hear from God? My family owns a couple hundred acres farm in the middle of nowhere for hunting in deer season. Our kids love to go fishing, hiking, and riding ATVs. It is a nice retreat away from all our busy lifestyle. But the problem is there is no cell phone service there.

When we are at home we have five bars of cell phone service reception. Most calls are received and you can communicate clearly back and forth. You can relay vital information, share exciting news, give or receive encouragement, share prayer requests, or just catch up with an old friend. But when we go visit our family, our cell phone reception goes from five bars to two bars of service. On two bars of reception, some calls may be dropped and there may be static during some conversations.

When we leave where our family lives and travel to the hunting cabin in the middle of nowhere, we go from two bars of cell phone service to zero bars of cell phone service. There is no cell phone reception in the middle of nowhere. No calls out and no calls in. No text messages. No social media. There are times when this can be a great thing. But it can also be a scary thing, not being able to contact someone in case of an emergency.

One day, I walked to every different room in the cabin to try to pick up a signal. I even once stood on one leg and stretched the phone as high as I could to try to get a signal. But nothing worked. Nothing I could have done would have helped. Why? We were too far away from the tower. Messages were being sent to me. Calls were being made to me, but I was out of range. The tower never moved but I had moved too far away from the tower.

Can I encourage you that messages are being sent and God is calling. Are you close enough to the tower to hear? Some people, who are too far away from the source, may say God does not speak any more. When we would leave the hunting cabin in the middle of nowhere and drive back towards our hometown, messages began to pop up, voice mails were received that came in while we were gone. Why? We were getting closer to the tower.

When I drove past where our family lives towards our home, the strength of signal grew stronger the closer I got to the tower. If you are away from God, take one step towards Him. The Bible says to "Draw near to God and He WILL draw near to you." God is waiting to speak to you. You have to make the first step.

START HERE ACTION STEPS

Pray at least 20 minutes every day. Start out praying five minutes, then ten, and so on. See prayer as a weight lifter, you have to gradually increase. Many Christians get discouraged and feel defeated because they can't pray an hour. Like the weight lifter, gradually over time - your prayer life will get stronger and longer. Remember: Don't focus on the time but on the heart!

START HERE SCRIPTURES

2 Chronicles 7:14

Philippians 4:6

James 5:16

Luke 18:1-14

1 Thess. 5:17

START HERE BIBLE MEMORIZATION

Jeremiah 33: 3 - 'Call to me and I will answer you and tell

you great and unsearchable things you do not know.'

START HERE DISCUSSION STARTERS

1. Why do some people find it hard to pray?

2. Why should we pray?

THE START HERE 20/20 CHALLENGE

I, _____ accept the "20/20

Challenge." I will set aside 20 minutes every day for prayer

and 20 minutes for reading and studying God's Word. I

make a commitment not only to God but to myself that I

might grow in my relationship with God and become a

true disciple.

_____ Date

_____ Signature

START HERE: BEGINNING WITH THE BASICS OF SPIRIT-FILLED FAITH

CHAPTER 3 - UNDERSTANDING YOUR SALVATION

"The salvation of a single soul is more important than the production or preservation of all the epics and tragedies in the world."

C.S. Lewis

Have you ever played golf? Do you remember the first time you played golf? I remember when a friend took me to play golf for the first time. I am no better today than I was then. I remember going to the first tee box and there was a group of more experienced golfers standing around watching. I was nervous; I had never hit a golf ball in front of other people except at the driving range. I teed

up my ball and acted like I knew what I was doing. I swung

the golf club as hard as I could and it flew…about fifteen

feet in front of the ladies' golf tee. My problem was I was

too close to the ball after I hit it.

I was so embarrassed but my friend looked at me

and said, "Don't worry take a mulligan." I said "What's a

mulligan?" He explained that a mulligan was a do-over or

second chance to hit again. I liked that idea, so I teed the

golf ball back up, with the crowd watching and hit the ball

50 yards. After a struggle, I eventually got the ball in the

cup and went on to the second hole.

Guess what happened? I hit the ball seventy five

yards and took another mulligan. Third hole, I hit into the

woods and you guessed it; I took another mulligan. This

golf stuff was not so hard after all. I shot a 100 for my first

golf outing, which really would have been 120 without all

the mulligans.

A few weeks later, a few friends asked me to go

golfing with them and I said, "Sure!" These guys were

better than my golf mentor, but on the first hole I

accidently hit a decent drive. Second hole, I hit a slice and

took my first mulligan. My friends laughed and said, "No

problem." Third hole, I hit into the water, and laughed and

then said I was going to take another mulligan.

My friends said, "Sorry but you only get one per

eighteen holes." I replied that I was told you could take

one every hole. I then realized that I didn't like golf

anymore. I believed something that my friend had taught

me that the rest of the world did not do. What you are taught and your beliefs are very important.

Many Christians struggle with condemnation because they do not fully understand their salvation. They know that they are set free and not going to hell but that is about it. This chapter we are going to look at what happens at salvation so we can fully understand it and be able to tell others.

First, let us look at how a person gets saved and then go from there. The best and simplest way I can explain it is with A-B-C.

You must first ADMIT that you are a sinner (Romans 3:23) and that Jesus died for your sins (Romans 5:8). Many do not think that they are a sinner, so they do not understand that they need Jesus. But the Bible says that we are all sinners! You may feel that you are a good person but just being a good person will not get you to heaven.

You must also BELIEVE that Jesus died for our sins to give us eternal life (Romans 6:23). Jesus died for our sins and rose again, giving us new life today and eternal life in the future.

Lastly, you must CONFESS with your mouth, Jesus as your Savior! (Romans 10:9-10, 13) When you prayed the prayer of salvation, you confessed Jesus as Lord.

Once we have admitted our sin, believed that Jesus died for our sins, and confessed Jesus as our Savior, how do we know that we have been "born again?" Some say that they felt a "burden" or heaviness lift off of them. Others felt a peace come over them. Some were filled with joy. Others say they really did not feel anything

special. No matter what type of experience you have, you

should not base your salvation on what you feel. The next

day the devil will try to tell you what happened was not

real and that is why you must have faith. Ephesians 2:8

says, "For by grace are ye saved through Faith; and that

not of yourselves: it is a gift of God."

What happens at salvation? Jesus gave us a new

covenant to live by. You can read in Hebrews 12:24 that

we no longer have to offer up sacrifices for our sins

because He became the sacrifice for our sins. This New

Covenant is so important because Adam's sin separated us

from God, under the Old Covenant. Before Christ's

resurrection, a priest would have to go in once a year on

the Day of Atonement and offer sacrifices for our sin. But

through the death of Jesus, the veil of the temple was torn

(Matt. 27:51), restoring the relationship between man and God the Father.

Let us look at this New Covenant in Ezekiel 36:25-27, "Then will I sprinkle clean water upon you, and ye shall be clean: from all your filthiness, and from all your idols, will I cleanse you. A new heart also will I give you, and a new spirit will I put within you: and I will take away the stony heart out of your flesh, and I will give you a heart of flesh. And I will put My spirit within you, and cause you to walk in My statutes, and ye shall keep My judgments, and do them."

We are washed from our sins.

The blood of Jesus cleanses us from all sin. (1 John 1:7) Titus 3:5 also states, "He saved us, not because of the righteous things we had done, but because of His mercy.

He washed away our sins, giving us a new birth and new life through the Holy Spirit." There is nothing you can do to remove your sins. We must be cleansed from our sins by the blood of Jesus.

We become a new creation.

Second Corinthians 5:17 states, "anyone who belongs to Christ has become a new person. The old life is gone; a new life has begun!" It stated in Ezekiel 36:26 that God would place a "new heart and new spirit" in us. If He just washed our sins away without placing a new heart in us, we would not be able to stay out of sin. But He places a new heart and outlook in our life. We now will see things differently than before and have more love in our hearts than before.

He places His Holy Spirit inside us.

Once we are cleansed from our sin and a new heart is placed in us, He seals us with His Holy Spirit. Ephesians 1:13 says, "And now you Gentiles have also heard the truth, the Good News that God saves you. And when you believed in Christ, he identified you as his own by giving you the Holy Spirit, whom he promised long ago."

The Holy Spirit is the "proof of purchase" or down-payment that He has purchased us through His Son's death. The Holy Spirit guides us and helps us follow His Word. He has sealed us with His Holy Spirit.

Many people confuse receiving the Holy Spirit at salvation and the Baptism of the Holy Spirit. They are two totally different experiences. We will discuss the Baptism of the Holy Spirit in the next chapter. The difference can be seen when the disciples received the Holy Spirit in John

20:21-22, before they were baptized in the Holy Spirit on the day of Pentecost.

I pray that now you understand what happened at your salvation better than before. We do not have space to get into everything because that would have filled a whole book in itself. Be sure to look up the study scriptures for an even better understanding.

At times Satan will try to convince you that you are not saved. He will say, "You are not saved. If you were really saved you would not have had a bad thought, said that word, or had the wrong attitude."

My Story

When I was a teenager, I used to work at K-Mart. I worked in the sporting goods department and would also have to gather buggies from the parking lot for future customers.

Every once in a while I would get the chance to help the plain clothes security officer watch potential thieves. They would have someone on camera sticking something in their pocket or purse. We would then have to trail them until they walked out of the store with the merchandise before we could bust them. Once I remember chasing a customer across our store parking lot as they tried to get away. One of our security team tackled the man with a stolen VCR player.

Why do I tell you about this? Because one day the tables were turned. Let me say that I do not remember ever stealing anything from a store, even as a child. One day I went to a local department store, I remember I was waiting on Beth as she shopped. I made a long trek all the way around the store in search of my wife. Then I stopped in the electronics department browsing the new movies when I saw it. I saw the department store security peeking around the end of an aisle watching me. It was strange having someone spy on me. Paranoia came over me and made me feel like I was suddenly a suspect on the FBI Most Wanted List. I pictured my mug shot on the news that night with the Words "Local Pastor Busted for Shoplifting."

Then I came back to reality and reminded myself that I had not done anything wrong. I quickly felt my pockets and smoothed them out to be sure I had not accidently put anything in them. They were empty. I was offended and wondered if I looked like someone who was a shoplifter. I left the electronics department and made my way towards the door. The security officer then began

to walk behind me. I got nervous and saw the

"merchandise detector" at the door of the store. I once

again double checked my pockets. As I got closer to the

front of the store I thought to myself, "Why am I upset? I

am innocent! I did not take anything. They have nothing

on me." The security guard then disappeared to another

aisle and was gone. He wasn't even after me. I walked out

the store but I had let my paranoia get to me and

condemn me even though I was innocent.

Can I encourage you that if you have accepted

Jesus Christ as your Savior and are following after Him,

Satan has nothing on you! He wants to condemn you and

to make you feel unsaved. He may whisper thoughts of "If

you were really saved you would not have thought that or

said that." The Bible states in Romans 8:1, "There is now

no condemnation for those who are in Christ Jesus, because through Christ Jesus the law of the Spirit who gives life has set you free from the law of sin and death." If a building is "condemned", it is unfit for use. Satan wants you to feel "unfit for use." Allow God to convict you of sin and repent, but never allow Satan to condemn you. You are washed from our sin.

START HERE ACTION STEPS

Begin to write down your testimony. A testimony is what God has done for you. Share what Jesus has done for you with someone you know. Continue to pray & study at least twenty minutes a day.

START HERE SCRIPTURES

Isaiah 53:3-5

John 3:16-17

Ephesians 2:4-10

Romans 8:15-17

Start Here Bible Memorization

2 Corinthians 5:17 – "Therefore, if anyone is in Christ, the new creation has come: The old has gone, the new is here!"

Start Here Discussion Starters

1. What must someone do to be saved?

2. Why should someone be saved?

Start Here: Beginning With the Basics of Spirit-Filled Faith

Chapter 4 - Receiving the Holy Spirit

"If you have not the Spirit of God, Christian worker, remember that you stand in somebody else's way; you are a fruitless tree standing where a fruitful tree might grow."

Charles Spurgeon

Speaking to a large audience, D.L. Moody held up a glass and asked, "How can I get the air out of this glass?" One man shouted, "Suck it out with a pump!" Moody replied, "That would create a vacuum and shatter the glass." After numerous other suggestions Moody smiled, picked up a pitcher of water, and filled the glass. "There,"

he said, "all the air is now removed." He then went on to

explain that victory in the Christian life is not accomplished

by "sucking out a sin here and there," but by being filled

with the Holy Spirit.[ii]

One of the most misunderstood parts of

Christianity is the person of the Holy Spirit. Many people

do not understand the working of the Holy Spirit, so they

just ignore Him. We must realize that the Holy Spirit is

essential to living a victorious life. There are a few basic

things we must understand.

The Holy Spirit is a person.

The Holy Spirit is not an "it" but the third part of

the Trinity. The Trinity is the Father, the Son (Jesus), and

the Holy Spirit. All three can be seen at the Baptism of

Jesus in Matthew 3:16-17. Jesus was baptized, the Holy

Spirit descended, and the Father spoke.

We do not serve three Gods but one God with

three distinct personalities. Deuteronomy 6:4 says, "Hear

O Israel: The Lord our God, the Lord is one!" The Holy

Spirit is just as much God, as the Father and the Son. That

would mean that the Holy Spirit has the same attributes as

would the Father and the Son. You can see the deity of

the Holy Spirit in the story of Ananias and Sapphira in Acts

5:1-4.

The Holy Spirit has many functions.

We must understand that the Holy Spirit does not

just float around in heaven but is active in the lives of

every believer. He helps us, comforts us, teaches us, and

guides us.

The Holy Spirit gives us power over sin.

Ezekiel 36:27 says, "And I will put my Spirit in you so that you will follow my decrees and be careful to obey my regulations." I know many people who still struggle with their walk with God. God said He would put His Spirit in us and the Holy Spirit would help us. In God's New Covenant, God no longer puts His Spirit just in building or temples, but we become the temple of the Holy Spirit (1 Corinthians 6:19). They Holy Spirit will not lead you commit sin but will help you do right. When you are facing times of temptation, say "Help me Holy Spirit."

The Holy Spirit gives you power to be a witness.

John 15:26, states that the Holy Spirit, "testifies of Jesus." God has not called us to be the judge but to be a witness. The Holy Spirit does not testify of Himself or a man but only of Jesus Christ. Everyone needs to have the "testifier" in them. Acts 1:8 says that we will "receive power" when the Holy Spirit comes upon us and we will tell people about Jesus everywhere.

The Holy Spirit will help you be bold when doors of opportunity open. Notice that the Holy Spirit brings power into our lives. The Greek word for power is "dunamis" which means explosive or TNT power. Explosive power is available to us as Christians. You don't have to be powerless.

The Holy Spirit gives power over struggles.

John 15:26 says, "When the Helper comes, whom I will send to you from the Father—the Spirit of truth who goes out from the Father—he will testify about me." The Holy Spirit is a Helper, Comforter, and Teacher for whatever situation that you face. He will speak to you and guide your steps. He is a helper who will never leave you. These are just a few of the main functions of the Holy Spirit

Before we receive Him, many of us need to unlearn some of the things we have been taught concerning the Holy Spirit. Some people were taught the Holy Spirit was of the devil. This is a lie from Satan. The Holy Spirit was sent from the Father. John 14:26 says, "But the Counselor, the Holy Spirit, whom the FATHER WILL SEND in my name, will teach you all things and will remind you of everything I have said to you." Look at how Peter's life was changed from before Pentecost to after Pentecost. The Holy Spirit made him closer to God. Satan opposes the Spirit. The Holy Spirit is to the devil what kryptonite is to superman. Who would want you to NOT receive the Holy Spirit?

You may need to unlearn that the Baptism of the Holy Spirit died with the disciples. It didn't die with the disciples. The Baptism of the Holy Spirit is available to ALL! Just take a quick look at Acts 2, when the Holy Spirit was poured out on the Jews and then in Acts 10 when it was poured out on us, the Gentiles. Acts 2:39 states, "The promise is for you and your children and for all who are far off--for all whom the Lord our God will call."

You might ask "Is the Baptism in the Holy Spirit really for me?" Joel 2:28 says, "I will pour out my Spirit on all people. Your sons and daughters will prophesy, your old men will dream dreams, your young men will see visions." God is NOT a respecter of persons! If He did it for them; He will do it for us.

You may need to unlearn that you do not need the Baptism of the Holy Spirit, because you received the Holy Spirit when you were saved. At salvation, the Holy Spirit draws you to Christ to save you! At salvation the Holy Spirit does reside within you. But the Baptism of the Holy Spirit is the second work of the Spirit in the life of a believer.

Read Acts 8:14-17 – "When the apostles in Jerusalem heard that Samaria had accepted the Word of God, they sent Peter and John to them. When they arrived, they prayed for them that they might receive the Holy Spirit, because the Holy Spirit had not yet come upon any of them; they had simply been baptized into the name of the Lord Jesus. Then Peter and John placed their hands on them, and they received the Holy Spirit."

Did you see that? The people of Samaria had accepted the Word, believed, and had already been baptized and then Peter and John laid hands on them to receive the Holy Spirit. Don't let your traditions or misunderstanding of scripture keep you from receiving ALL God has for you.

How does someone receive the power of the Holy Spirit?

As we discussed in the last lesson, we receive the Holy Spirit, when we first get saved. We become born of the Spirit when we ask Jesus to come into our heart and life (John 3:5). Jesus comes and lives in our heart in the person of the Holy Spirit. (Romans 8:9) But there is a difference from receiving the Holy Spirit and being baptized in the Holy Spirit. To receive the Baptism of the Holy Spirit, you must first understand that it is a gift. There is nothing you can do to earn it or deserve it. Peter proclaimed in Acts 2:39, "The promise is for you and your children and for all who are far off—for all whom the Lord our God will call."

Once you have repented of your sins, you must ask God to fill you with the Holy Ghost. Matthew 5:6 says, "Blessed are those who hunger and thirst for righteousness, for they will be filled." If you ask God and are serious about seeking the Baptism in the Holy Spirit, you will be filled. Some people say, "If God wanted me to have the Baptism of the Holy Spirit, He would have given it to me," but just like you asked God for your salvation, you must also ask to be filled. The Holy Spirit is gentle and will never force Himself where He is not invited.

My Story

When I was around twenty years old, I helped lead a group of youth to a major Christian event in Washington, DC. We were so excited because on the schedule for the event was a popular evangelist. We talked most of the way there about the evangelist praying a prayer over us and the blessing we might receive.

We stopped and spent the night at a local church and slept in their gymnasium. The next morning we awoke early to get as close to the stage as we could for the all day event. We had a great time during the day listening to Christian music and inspiring speakers, but we were anticipating something extraordinary happening that evening when the popular evangelist spoke.

The time we had all been waiting on had finally arrived. It was the evangelist's time to speak. He came onto the stage and gave everyone in the audience an encouraging word and then commenced to pray for us all. We were excited to receive prayer from this mighty man of God. We raised our hands in worship to God and he prayed... and he prayed. I remember opening my eyes and peeking. I looked at the evangelist but felt nothing. I thought to myself, "I rode on a school bus without air conditioning for eight hours with thirty teens for this?"

The event ended and I could tell that I wasn't the only one who was disappointed. I wasn't disappointed in the evangelist but I was disappointed in myself. I was so caught up in the moment and fixed my eyes on man instead of God. I believe we should respect and show honor to God's servants but they must not become our source. On the bus ride home, no one said a word. Everyone was disappointed and exhausted.

We stopped for a quick dinner and then went back to the gym of the local church. We gathered the group of young people for a short bible study and worship. As soon as we began to worship God, the presence of God filled that small gym. We began to pray for one another and that night I received that night from God, what I expected to receive from the evangelist that day. God radically changed my life that night when I put my focus on Him.

How will I know when I have received the Holy Spirit?

Every instance in Acts, when people were baptized in the Holy Spirit, the initial evidence was that they began to speak with other tongues. When those on the day of Pentecost were filled with the Holy Ghost, the Bible states "All of them were filled with the Holy Spirit and began to speak in other tongues as the Spirit enabled them." (Acts 2:4) You will know when you have fully received the Holy

Spirit, when you begin to speak with other tongues. It is not a language which can be learned or taught, but which is only given when a person receives the gift of the Holy Spirit.

Those in the Bible also received boldness to witness when they received the Holy Spirit. We will discuss in the next lesson, about using that boldness for the great commission and sharing our faith.

START HERE ACTION STEPS

Continue to set aside daily time to pray for 20 minutes and 20 for studying and reading God's Word. Continue reading a chapter in Proverbs a day and begin to read one chapter of Psalms a day. If you have not received the Baptism of the Holy Spirit, begin to seek after it and ask God for it!

START HERE SCRIPTURES

Acts 2:1-4

Eph. 3:20

Acts 2:39

Acts 10:44-48

START HERE BIBLE MEMORIZATION

Acts 1:8 – "But you will receive power when the Holy Spirit comes on you; and you will be my witnesses in Jerusalem, and in all Judea and Samaria, and to the ends of the earth."

START HERE DISCUSSION STARTERS

1. Why should someone be filled with the Holy Ghost?

2. How will you know when you've received the Holy Ghost?

START HERE: BEGINNING WITH THE BASICS OF SPIRIT-FILLED FAITH

CHAPTER 5 – ACCEPTING THE GREAT COMMISSION AND THE GREAT COMMANDMENT

"The Great Commission is not an option to be considered; it is a command to be obeyed."

Hudson Taylor

Susan was in tears. She had just seen a report about another gang related crime in her city. She began to ask God, "When are you going to do something about this?" A still small voice said, "That's why I sent you."

In the last chapter, we discussed how to receive the Holy Spirit and His power in our lives. This chapter we will discover what God wants us to do with that power. The Bible says that we will be witnesses for Christ after the Holy Spirit has come upon us! We do not receive the Holy Spirit just to make us feel better, but to make an impact on others with the Gospel of Jesus Christ.

As we discussed in the last chapter, you cannot be an effective witness until you have received the Holy Spirit. The Holy Spirit in our lives changes our focus from ourselves to others. This outward focus can be sensed when Jesus gave us the Great Commission and the Great Commandment.

In Matthew 28:29-20, God gives us this Great Commission, and it states, "Go therefore, and teach all nations, baptizing them in the name of the Father, and the Son, and of the Holy Ghost: teaching them to observe all things whatsoever I have commanded you: and lo, I am with you always, even unto the end of the world." Jesus calls all His disciples to go to people of all nations and teach them how to know and live for Him.

We are not to wander aimlessly without purpose throughout life. Through this Great Commission, God gives clear direction and purpose for our lives. He has given us a mission and that makes everyone of us a missionary. You do not have to go to Africa to be a missionary. You can be a missionary in your community, at school, and at work. While Jesus was on Earth, He was on a mission to "seek and save" those who were lost. Now He has commissioned us to do likewise.

The Great Commandment can be found in
Matthew 22: 37-40. It says, "You shall love the Lord your
God with all your heart, with all your soul, and with all
your mind. This is the first and great commandment. And
the second is like it: You shall love your neighbor as
yourself. On these two commandments hang all the law
and all the prophets." This is a commandment not a
recommendation. This commandment consists of two
things: loving God and loving people. If we love others, we
will share the Gospel with them.

Just because Jesus told us to "go and preach" in the
Great Commission, it does not mean everyone will. We
must have the "love" that is talked about in the Great
Commandment! If you obey the Great Commandment
then you will have no problem obeying the Great
Commission. If you love God with all you heart, soul, and

mind, then you will have love for others. If you don't love God, you can't fully love others. The love that we should have for others stems from our love for God. Without a passion for God, we cannot have true compassion for anyone. And likewise, we do not truly love God if we do not love people.

When you have a love for people, you want to share Jesus with them and show them the love of God. Many people feel overwhelmed by the Great Commission, but once we realize that we have been filled with the Holy Spirit and the love of God, nothing can stop us. Will you accept this Great Commission to "go and be a witness" and the Great Commandment, to "love God with all your heart, soul, and mind and love others"?

My Story

I do not eat much ice cream but a few years ago, a friend told me that I had to try "Cold Stone Creamery" ice cream. My friend said it was the best ice cream he had ever eaten. I was hungry for ice cream once he described his ice cream creation. At Cold Stone Creamery, you can add any flavor combinations you want and build your own creation. I am getting hungry as I think about it.

A few days later, Beth and I were on a date, and we just had to stop at Cold Stone Creamery to see what the buzz was all about. We opened the door and the wonderful smells of the different fresh fruit toppings and brownies hit us. We knew we were going to like it. We walked up to the counter and they had dozens of delicious toppings. I felt like a kid in a candy store. Someone in front of us was getting candy sprinkles, fruit, and chocolate syrup added to theirs.

On the menu board they had a dozen or more Signature Creations that they recommended, but one of them caught my attention. It was called the "Birthday Cake Remix Ice Cream Creation." The Birthday Cake Remix included cake batter ice cream, a brownie, chocolate syrup, fudge, and candy sprinkles. They asked, "Would you like a sample?" I agreed, and they put some on a very small spoon just enough to entice me. I put the small spoon in my mouth and it was heavenly. The cake batter ice cream mixed with a brownie, which was perfectly mixed with the chocolate syrup, and then the sprinkles. It was like I was eating a frozen piece of birthday cake, only better.

My wife and I placed our orders. She got her own because I was not going to share. (Smile!) We slowly enjoyed each bite of our ice cream creations until the cup was completely empty. I remember leaving the store and immediately thinking, "I have to tell someone about this." I called some family members that evening and told them that they needed to try the Birthday Cake Remix at Cold Stone Creamery. Later that weekend, I told most of my friends how much I enjoyed the experience.   Many of them later went themselves to experience the Birthday Cake Remix and loved it, and in return told someone else.

What happened? We found out about something good, experienced it ourselves, and told other people. We shared the good news about Cold Stone Creamery and people followed our lead. They went on to experience it. If we would do that for ice cream, our favorite restaurant, or a new movie, why would we not do that with the Gospel of Jesus? Psalm 34:8 says, "Taste and see that the LORD is good." Once we have experienced Jesus and have seen that He is good, we need to tell other people. I once heard someone describe witnessing as one beggar telling another beggar where there is free bread.

One of my wife's first jobs as a teenager was that she was the "Sample, Sample!" lady at the mall for Chick-Fil-A. She didn't have to do anything but pass out samples of chicken to passerbys. Did the FREE sample, make people hungry? Absolutely! When was the last time you made anyone hungry for more of God? When there are open doors you should share the Good News, your story, and your testimony. God has commanded and commissioned us to share the Good News around the world. I hope I made you hungry today!

Begin to pray and ask God to fill you with the love of God and give you a love for Him and for others that you might do what He is calling you to do.

START HERE ACTION STEPS

Continue to pray at least 20 minutes a day and study 20 minutes a day. Reading at least one chapter in the New Testament, one chapter of Proverbs, and one Psalm every day. Share your faith to at least one person this week.

START HERE SCRIPTURES

Matt. 9:35-36

Luke 24:44-49

1 Corinthians 13

START HERE BIBLE MEMORIZATION

John 3:16 – "For God so loved the world that He gave his one and only Son, that whoever believes in Him shall not perish but have eternal life."

START HERE DISCUSSION STARTERS

1.   Does God want us to love everybody? Explain.

2.   What keeps some people from not sharing their faith?

START HERE
Beginning with the Basics of Spirit-Filled Faith

Chapter 6 – Starting to Serve

"The first question which the priest and the Levite asked

was: "If I stop to help this man, what will happen to me?"

But the Good Samaritan reversed the question: "If I do not

stop to help this man, what will happen to him?"

Martin Luther King Jr

Beth's grandmother Faye was a wonderful cook.

During Christmas time it was a tradition to have a large

feast of food. The family would gather and she would fix a

large ham, mashed potatoes, green beans, corn, macaroni and cheese, casseroles, candy, and desserts. She would work for days preparing the ingredients, cooking desserts, and cooking all her delicious foods. The day of the feast she would get up early and cook all morning until the afternoon. We would walk into the house and it smelled delicious.

Finally family members would arrive and after a short visit we would all gather around the table and say grace. We would then walk around the table like we were on a carousel filling our plates high with the delicious food. Everyone would then pick their spots to eat. One Christmas, I noticed that while we were all eating Beth's grandmother wasn't eating at all but was watching us all enjoy her creations. I was immediately concerned, I wondered if she was feeling sick or just exhausted from her labors. I remembered asking her "Faye, Are you feeling okay? Come and eat with us." She replied, "I am fine. I am just not hungry." It surprised me that someone who cooked so much wouldn't eat her own cooking.

I thought about it for the rest of the day and even shared my concern with my wife, Beth. I made a mental note that I would investigate the situation again next year. The following Christmas season we arrived before anyone else showed up. I received a "behind the scene" look at Grandma Faye's feast producing factory. I was amazed to watch her sample all her creations while she was cooking them. She would take a spoonful of mashed potatoes, a pinch of ham, a sample of green beans, macaroni, and so on.

I found out the reason that Faye wasn't hungry during the meal was that she would eat first! She ate more than a plate of food before it ever hit the table. She could not eat another bite if she wanted to. I learned a powerful lesson that day that the one who serves others will eat first. If you want to be fed, serve people. We get fed by serving and doing the Will of God. Jesus said His food was to do the Will of God. If you teach a small group, you will have to "eat first" before you can share your lesson. If you preach, you will have to feed yourself the Word God, before you share it. You can only give what you have received.

We live in a day where we are accustomed to focusing on ourselves. Ads in magazines say you deserve that new expensive watch, the luxury car, and that new wardrobe. It's all about you! But in the Kingdom of God that's not the case. God wants us to be focused on meeting the needs of others!

In the world, people strive for greatness and power by being over people. In the Kingdom of God greatness is serving! In the world, greatness is having people serve you; but in God's kingdom greatness is serving others. Mark 10:43-45 states, "...but whosoever will be great among you, shall be your servant: and whosoever of you will be the chiefest, shall be servant of all. For even the Son of man came not to be ministered unto, but to serve, and give his life a ransom for many. "

God wants you to be great! And you can be great by serving! God did not call us to be someone's slave but to be a servant. A servant is someone that helps others, ministers to them, and meets their needs.

Many people used to wear WWJD (What Would Jesus Do) bracelets and didn't know what Jesus did. Jesus became a servant! It said in Mark 10, He did not come to be served but to serve. If Jesus became a servant, don't you think we should, too?

Philippians 2:5-8 says, "Let this mind be in you, which was also in Christ Jesus: Who, being in the form of God, thought it not robbery to be equal with God: But made himself of no reputation, and took upon him the form of a servant, and was made in the likeness of men: and being found in fashion as a man, he humbled himself, and became obedient unto death, even the death of the cross." Paul encourages us here to have the mind of a servant, the mind of Christ. Jesus didn't come to earth to establish a reputation for himself because He was already the Son of God.

He did not try to impress anyone, but He became a servant. The King of Kings and Lord of Lords emptied Himself of His heavenly privileges and became a servant. Jesus set the example for us to follow! We are to have that same mindset of unselfishness and service to others.

Ephesians 6:6-7 states, "Not with eyeservice, as men pleasers: but as the servants of Christ, doing the will of God from the heart; with good will doing service, as to the Lord, and not to men." God wants us to serve, not just to please people or to make us look good; He wants us to do it from our heart. God wants everything that we do to glorify Him!   Even if you are asked to serve by cleaning we should do everything as if we are doing it for God.

The true mark of maturity in Christ is when you become outward focused. We are called to not just see the needs but to meet the needs. You will begin to

discover, as you bless others, God will begin to bless you.

Ask God to give you the mind of Christ, where you are not

just focused on yourself but on others. Start to look for

needs and begin meeting those needs and search for ways

that you can serve God.

My Story

Our church is very involved in serving the homeless

in our city. We have a group that started from our church

called the "River City Love Squad". RCLS feeds, clothes,

and ministers to the homeless every week. Our church

goes once a month and takes food. Our musicians and

singers hold a worship service for them.

I remember the first time I was there, I was asked

to speak. I had prayed all week about what I was to speak

on, and on the day of the service God whispered that I was to wash their feet. I love these people but I am not a feet person. God wanted me to humble myself and serve these wonderful people that He loved. He told me I was to tell them that they may feel forgotten but God loves them and I was to prove it to them.

When it was time for me to speak, I stepped up to the microphone and told them, "God loves you and I am going to show you. God asked me to wash your feet." Everyone in attendance began to squirm. I begin to share how Jesus washed the disciples' feet as an act of service and I was there to serve them. Out of the crowd of almost sixty homeless people, only a handful stood up to be the first in line but the others just waited and watched.

One by one they began to peel off their socks and showed feet covered with sores and blisters from shoes being too tight. They begin to stick their feet in the cool water, and I would wash them and pray over each person. Many began to weep. Our team then followed and grabbed a tub of water and found someone to serve. Before it was over, almost everyone had their feet washed and received ministry. God really touched many hearts that night including mine. One man shared with me that no one had ever washed his feet, and that he had been set free that night.

I am not sharing this so you will think I am a special person. But to show every one of us can do something special for others if we are willing to serve. Humble yourself and start serving today.

START HERE ACTION STEPS

Continue our 20/20 Daily Challenge. Look for ways to

serve God everyday by helping others. Do a random act of

serving.

START HERE SCRIPTURES

Matt. 25:14-46

Mark 10:42-46

Romans 12:1-2

Philippians 2:5-8

START HERE BIBLE MEMORIZATION

Mark 10:43 – "Whoever wants to become great among you must be your servant."

START HERE SERVING

I served God today by:

Monday:

Tuesday:

Wednesday:

Thursday:

Friday:

Saturday:

Sunday:

START HERE DISCUSSION STARTERS

1.   What keeps you from serving?

2.   What is one act of service that you can do?

START HERE
BEGINNING WITH THE BASICS OF SPIRIT-FILLED FAITH

CHAPTER 7 – STEWARDSHIP

"I have observed 100,000 families over my years of investment counseling. I always saw greater prosperity and happiness among those families who tithed than among those who didn't."

-John Templeton, Chairman of Templeton Funds

I love to take my daughters on daddy dates. They get all dressed up. We will then go out to see a movie that they picked. One particular time, I took them out and we enjoyed the movie. I then took them shopping and bought each of them a new pair of shoes. I completed the date by letting them pick where they wanted to eat. To my amazement, they both quickly responded "Taco Bell"! It was their pick so I obliged.

Since we were going somewhere inexpensive, I let them choose whatever they wanted. They both ordered different things from the menu but agreed we had to have cinnamon twists. Cinnamon twists are crispy, puffed corn twists, sprinkled with cinnamon and sugar. I placed my order then we sat down to eat. We had great conversation about what was happening at school and enjoyed our time together. Once we finished our meal, we were all ready to devour the cinnamon twists. I grabbed one and they both quickly grabbed the bag and said, "Get your own!"

I had taken the girls on a daddy date, took them shopping, blessed them with new shoes, and provided the food and cinnamon twists. But they wouldn't even think of sharing with their dad a small portion. How many times do we act this way towards God?

You might read the title of this lesson and ask, "What is stewardship?" Stewardship is taking care of what you have, whether it is money, time, or life. Everything that we have comes from God. He has blessed us and given us the ability to work. We are just managers or stewards of His blessings.

In this chapter, we are going to discuss what the Bible say we are to do with our money as a Christian. If we are not good stewards of our finances, then we will have financial problems which will put a strain on our spiritual life!

The Bible says a lot about money and what to do with it. Proverbs 22:6-7 says, "Train up a child...the borrower is servant to the lender." God wants us to teach even our children about finances. Why? Oswald Sanders, once said, "Money is one of the acid tests of character and a surprising amount of space is given to it in Scripture...Whether a man is rich or poor, observe his reaction to his possessions and you have a revealing index to his character." Money is not the root of all evil but the LOVE of money is the root of all evil. (I Timothy 6:10)

The first thing we must do with our money as a Christian is tithe. To tithe means "to give one tenth or 10% of all your gross earnings." This is before taxes or other bills. Malachi 3:10 states, "Bring ye ALL the tithes into the storehouse, that there may be meat in mine house, and prove me now wherewith, saith the Lord of Hosts, if I will not open the windows of heaven, and pour you out a blessing, that there shall not be room enough to receive it."

The Bible said, "Bring your tithes" into the storehouse. The Bible teaches us that the tithe (ten percent of your gross income) belongs in the storehouse -- the local church. I can't find examples in the Bible of people giving the tithe outside the church, temple, or to the priest. I therefore cannot "tithe" to just any organization including "Save the Animals" or a televangelist. The Bible teaches that I can give an offering to other organizations but my tithe belongs in the local church.

Giving your tithes is a blessing not a burden. When we tithe, God blesses us and we can do more with 90% than we could have with 100%. You might wonder, "If God doesn't need my money why should I tithe?" God wants us to tithe to show that we trust Him in all aspects of our life. When we tithe, we are trusting Him and realizing that everything that we have is from Him.

Proverbs 3:9-10 states "Honor the Lord with your possessions and with the first fruits of all your increase; so your barns will be filled with plenty, and your vats will overflow with new wine." Some people say that tithing isn't for today that it was under the "old covenant." But tithing was around at least 400 years before the old covenant was given. Abraham gave a tithe to the priest Melchizedek. (Genesis 14:20)

Secondly, we must give offerings. Offerings are anything above your tithe. It is not the dollar amount you give that matters but how you give. It's not about the total but about the sacrifice. You may not be able to give the same amount as someone else but you can make an equal sacrifice. In Luke Chapter 21, there was a widow who gave only two mites which wasn't much compared to everyone else, who gave large amounts. Jesus said she had given more than the rest because she gave her all. The others gave what was left. God wants us to give our best not just what is left.

Finally, we must give alms to the poor. The Bible is clear that we are to help the poor by giving them "alms". Alms does not mean tithe. Alms were small amounts of money used for a meal. You cannot tithe to your son, daughter, mom, dad, brother, or sister. Our tithe cannot pay their rent, electric bill, etc. We should help them but that is not our tithe. Martin Luther once said, "God divided the hands into the fingers so that money could slip through them." We must take care of those who are without. I John 3:17 states, "If someone has enough money to live well and sees a brother or sister in need but shows no compassion—how can God's love be in that person?"

My Story

My wife, Beth, and I have always tithed. Our pastor taught us to tithe as teenagers. As teenagers, we would make $100 week and give a tithe to God of $10. We believed God's Word and our children have seen us tithe. Since they were six or seven, they would ask if they could tithe off their birthday money received from their family and friends. We would never discourage them from it.

One year, Stephen was around eight years old and received around one hundred dollars from his grandparents for his birthday. That weekend, he had spent $90 of his birthday money on toys. He had saved ten dollars for his tithe of the one hundred and put it in a church tithe envelop. That particular Sunday we had a guest evangelist at the church and in the foyer he sold t-shirts, CDs, and books. Stephen looked through all the t-shirts and found one that he wanted. He was in a dilemma. He knew his tithe was ten dollars and the t-shirt was ten dollars. Could he save his tithe and buy the shirt that he wanted? We let him decide. Even though he really wanted the shirt, he decided to give his money in the offering to God.

After the service, he went out to the tables of merchandise in the foyer and scanned over the shirts one last time. No one else knew of his decision to give. The evangelist then told Stephen to pick out any shirt that He wanted for FREE! Stephen was so excited and learned a powerful lesson as a child to give.

He has since tithed off of his birthday money every year. One year he used his birthday money to buy a cheap electric guitar at the pawn shop. On Sunday, he went to church and gave his tithe on his own. That evening a friend visited us, and Stephen proudly pulled out his new electric guitar to show him. The friend asked, "Do you have an amp yet?" Stephen replied, "Not yet." Our friend said "I have a large guitar amp at my house that I never use. Would you like it?" Stephen smiled knowing what God had done and said "Absolutely!"

We must take care of what God has blessed us with. God gives to us according to our ability to receive. If we are not good stewards of what God has given us, why should God bless us with more?

START HERE ACTION STEPS

Increase your 20/20 Time. Begin to consistently tithe for the next 90 days & watch what God will do.

START HERE SCRIPTURES

Malachi 3:10-11

Matthew 22:21

Proverbs 3:9-10

Proverbs 22:6-7

START HERE BIBLE MEMORIZATION

Mal. 3:10 – "Bring the whole tithe into the storehouse, that there may be food in my house. Test me in this," says the LORD Almighty, "and see if I will not throw open the floodgates of heaven and pour out so much blessing that there will not be room enough to store it."

START HERE DISCUSSION STARTERS

1. Why should someone "tithe" or give offerings?

2. Why do some people not "tithe" or give to God?

START HERE CONCLUSION

This may be the end of this book but it is just the beginning of your journey. You may be a new Christian or someone who just wanted a refresher course on the basics. Wherever you are in your spiritual growth, remember the goal is to not only start well but to also finish well. In this race, you will face many mountains and some valleys but take your race one day at a time. My challenge to you is to take what you've learned and grow.

I have given you the tools to start the race and finish it, but you must make a personal decision to apply what you have learned. The Bible calls us to be doers of the Word not just hearers only (James 1:22). If you only read this book and do not apply the Word of God to your life, you will not have strength for the race. Your spiritual life is only as strong as what it rests on.

In Matthew 7, Jesus tells the story of two people that each built a house. One man built his house on the rock and one man built his house on the sand. Listen to how Jesus describes the man who built on a solid foundation. "Anyone who listens to my teaching and follows it is wise, like a person who builds a house on solid rock. Though the rain comes in torrents and the floodwaters rise and the winds beat against that house, it won't collapse because it is built on bedrock. "(Vs. 25-26)

When we build our lives on the Word of God and obey it, we are building our lives on stable ground. Our economy and society may seem unstable but we can be secure by following God's Word. It takes effort to have a stable spirit filled life. 2 Peter 1:5 says for us to "make every effort to respond to God's promises." You do your part and I guarantee God will do His part.

Have you ever experienced pressure from every side? You are not alone! Jesus tells the disciples that the storm came to both houses. They both experienced pressure from above in the rain. They both experienced pressure from the side in the wind.   They both experienced pressure from below in the flood. But only one stood after the storm.   You will know you are standing on the rock, if you are standing after the storm.

Someone might ask "Why should I serve God if I am going to face the same storms as everyone else?" My answer is that we have a secure future with God when we build our foundation on the rock. Make a commitment today to not only start the race but to finish the race.

Grow everyday in your relationship with God and one day

you will be able to stand like Paul and say "I have fought

the good fight, I have finished the race, and I have

remained faithful."

START HERE ENDNOTES

Introduction

1. How the Best Leaders Lead by Brian Tracy

Chapter 4

2. D.L. Moody Quote. - *Today in the Word*, September, 1991, p. 30.

ABOUT THE AUTHOR

Joshua Sargent is Lead Pastor of Good Shepherd Worship Center in Louisville, KY. He is best known for his communication of practical, biblical principles. Joshua and his wife, Beth, have three children, Stephen, Sophia, and Sarah. They live in Mount Washington, KY.

FIFTH INNING
FADE-OUT

Sports Books by C. PAUL JACKSON

For younger boys:

BIG PLAY IN THE SMALL LEAGUE
CHRIS PLAYS SMALL FRY FOOTBALL
LITTLE LEAGUE TOURNAMENT
LITTLE MAJOR LEAGUER
FIFTH INNING FADE-OUT
PEE WEE COOK OF THE MIDGET LEAGUE
STEPLADDER STEVE PLAYS BASKETBALL
TIM, THE FOOTBALL NUT
TOM MOSELY—MIDGET LEAGUER
TOMMY, SOAP BOX DERBY CHAMPION
TWO BOYS AND A SOAP BOX DERBY

For older boys:

BASEBALL'S SHRINE
BUD BAKER, COLLEGE PITCHER
BUD BAKER, HIGH SCHOOL PITCHER
BUD BAKER, RACING SWIMMER
BUD PLAYS JUNIOR HIGH BASKETBALL
BUD PLAYS JUNIOR HIGH FOOTBALL
BUD PLAYS SENIOR HIGH BASKETBALL
BULLPEN BARGAIN
FULLBACK IN THE LARGE FRY LEAGUE
HALFBACK!
HALL OF FAME FLANKERBACK
JUNIOR HIGH FREESTYLE SWIMMER
PASS RECEIVER
PENNANT STRETCH DRIVE
MINOR LEAGUE SHORTSTOP
PRO FOOTBALL ROOKIE
PRO HOCKEY COMEBACK
ROOKIE CATCHER WITH THE ATLANTA BRAVES
ROSE BOWL PRO
SECOND TIME AROUND ROOKIE
SUPER MODIFIED DRIVER
WORLD SERIES ROOKIE

FIFTH INNING FADE-OUT

by

C. PAUL JACKSON

Illustrated by Floyd James Torbert

HASTINGS HOUSE, PUBLISHERS

NEW YORK

Library of Congress Cataloging in Publication Data
Jackson, Caary Paul,
  Fifth inning fade-out.
  SUMMARY: Joe's position as pitcher for his
Khoury League team is threatened because he always falls
apart after four innings.
  [1. Baseball—Stories]   I. Torbert, Floyd James
illus.   II. Title.

PZ7.J1322Fi   [Fic]   73-39117
ISBN 0-8038-2287-1

Library of Congress Catalogue Card Number: 73-39117
Printed in the United States of America

Contents

	A Note About	
	the Khoury League	7
Chapter One	Fact, No Brag	13
Chapter Two	There Is More	
	Than One Position	26
Chapter Three	Collision	34
Chapter Four	But Not *This* Position!	45
Chapter Five	Second Half Opening Game	55
Chapter Six	Some Kind of Jinx?	66
Chapter Seven	Two Games—One Rained Out	75
Chapter Eight	Television Appearance	85
Chapter Nine	At the Supermarket	99
Chapter Ten	Federal Versus Dinner	109
Chapter Eleven	Fact, No Brag!	117

A Note about the Khoury League

THIS STORY is about a boy who plays in one of the Khoury Baseball Leagues. These started in the summer of 1937, when George Khoury and his wife organized and sponsored two leagues of youngsters in their neighborhood—eight teams that played their games on a lot in South St. Louis.

What began as "just a neighborhood league," has since grown into a national network of thousands of Khoury League teams extending into many states.

Now in its third decade, the Khoury association is a non-profit, non-denominational organization of affiliated circuits, or leagues, using a hub-system of control and administration. It is designed to administer anything from one four-team league to a network of leagues.

The national office in St. Louis serves as an administrative, advisory headquarters. Each individual community, however, elects its own officers and administers its own affairs.

There is no financial profit in the Khoury association—only the profit of clean fun and character-building recreation received by the boys. The Khoury association has nothing to sell but good will. Its program has won the support and endorsement of city officials, civic, fraternal and spiritual leaders, and sportswriters.

Khoury League Atom Class is for boys 7–8 years of age; Bantam Class for boys 9–10; Midget Class 11–12; Juvenile for boys 13–14; Junior Class players are from the 15–16 age group.

Dinner batting order and roster

Coach, Walt Smith

Batting order

Pete Inglis	ss
Dave Hammer	cf
Harry Tessario	1b
Bill Smith	c
Joe Mancin	p
Tom Dancer	lf
Fred Cook	rf
Jim Kubelik	3b
Lon Alfo	2b

Reserves

Mike Ortega	p
Paul Orton	p
Dick Thomas	of
Hank Strome	if
Forest Ennis	p
Red Bennett	of
Carlos Vardez	batboy, cheerleader,

FIFTH INNING
FADE-OUT

CHAPTER ONE

Fact, No Brag

"BALL FOUR!"

The batter threw his bat toward the dugout and started for first base at the umpire's call. A base runner from first trotted to second. The catcher fired the ball at the left-handed pitcher and yelled, "Settle down! Make 'em hit to get on!"

Joe Mancin stood back of the pitcher's slab, a moroseness in his dark eyes as he watched the Federal batter coming to the plate. He lifted his cap and wiped his shirt sleeve over his sweat-curled black hair, then settled the cap firmly. Trying desperately to keep from thinking sour thoughts, Joe ran his fingers across the lettering on his shirt. D-I-N-N-E-R.

Coach Smith had explained this odd team name to Joe when he issued his uniform: "It goes back quite a few years," he said. "The Broward County Diner sponsored a team in the first Khoury League that was organized around here. Whoever typed the order for the uniforms hit the "n" key twice by mistake, so the uniforms came marked with DINNER rather than DINER. There was no time to return the shirts before the first game so they wore them.

"That first "Dinner" team started right in beating the ears off every team in their league and it soon became a tradition—maybe a superstition—for Diner teams to be called Dinner teams."

Somebody in the stands shouted, "Get on with the game!"

Joe Mancin picked the ball out of his glove and chunked it into the pocket. Dinner, breakfast, lunch, supper or whatever, Joe Mancin was making hash of this game for his team.

This was the fifth time he had pitched well—actually *real* well—for four innings. It was also the fifth time that rival batters began getting to him, either working him for bases on balls, or clobbering his left-handed offerings after four innings. Was he going to come unglued again?

"Whip that ole ball up here!" Bill Smith, chunky Dinner catcher, chattered behind the plate. "Zero that ole apple in at the target!"

A slender boy with brown skin, warm brown eyes and straight black hair, stood in the dugout and yelled, "Give it to him, Joe-kid. Pour on the coal, Big Joe!"

"Make him quit stalling, Ump!" The shout was from a boy on the Federal bench. "Tell 'im to throw it up there and duck!"

Joe recognized the Federal pitcher. The shout did not rattle him and Joe felt an odd sympathy for the Federal boy when his coach turned and frowned at him. Bill Smith crouched behind the plate and gave a sign.

Joe nodded, toed the pitching rubber and glanced at base runners on first and second. Then he put all he had behind the pitch—and sucked in a breath the instant the ball left his hand.

Smith's mitt was held a little above the letters of the batter and off the inside edge of the plate. But the ball was a long way from the "zero that ole apple in on the target" that the catcher wanted. It was a nothing-pitch right down the middle of the strike zone and belt high.

Timing his swing perfectly, the batter brought his bat around smoothly, and seasoned ash cracked against speeding horsehide. A fuzzy white streak sizzled over the second baseman's head and into right center field. Only the quickness of Dave Hammer kept the solidly hit drive from going for extra bases.

The speedy Dinner centerfielder dashed across, grabbed the ball on the second hop and almost in the same motion drilled it to Lon Alfo, who had run ten yards out from his second base position.

Lon's fine peg to Bill Smith at home plate made the runner rounding third put on the brakes and dive back to the bag. But now the bases were loaded.

Coach Smith, a stocky man with sandy hair and keen blue eyes, came from the Dinner dugout. He signalled the umpire for time to be called and walked slowly to the pitcher's mound. Joe was fully aware of the boys who hustled from the dugout to the Dinner bullpen. Bill Smith came from behind the plate. He gave a slight shrug as his father looked questioningly at him.

"He's still got good stuff," the catcher said. "He just ain't wheeling that thing in there where I call for it!"

"Isn't." Coach Walt Smith made the correction automatically. He regarded Joe Mancin.

"Are you tired?" the coach asked.

Joe shook his head.

Smith said, "Your arm sore or anything like that?"

"I feel fine!" Joe wailed. "Nothing's the matter except the blamed ball just doesn't go where I aim it!"

"Baseballs have that peculiar bent sometimes for pitchers, son." The skin at the corners of Walt Smith's eyes crinkled and he nodded. "It's called loss of control, and it is nothing to laugh about. Keep in mind, though, that I have been coaching youngsters a good many years. You are not the first pitcher I've had with control trouble, and the probabilities are you won't be the last."

The coach held Joe's eyes steadily. "We don't want it to become a habit," he said, "and I'm sure you will eventually work out of it. But it is no good to try to fool me, or yourself. If you honestly feel that you can get these fellows out, I'll leave you in. If you have lost your confidence, we'd better get you off the mound quick-like!"

Joe set his jaw. "I want to stay in," he said. "I can get 'em out!"

Then when the coach nodded and turned toward the dugout, Joe wondered if he could.

No pitcher ever tried harder to throw where his catcher held the mitt-target. His first effort was a little off, but still nicked a corner of the plate and earned the umpire's strike call. Then the big left-hander missed the strike zone badly with three consecutive pitches. A three-and-one count; he had to get the next one in the strike zone, or force a run across the plate. But not too good, not another fat nothing-pitch.

Joe tried to focus on Bill Smith's mitt, but as he toed the rubber he could not help seeing that the boys in the bullpen were throwing more rapidly.

His pitch was away wide outside the batter's

box on the first base side of the plate, and so low that it hit the dirt as Bill Smith dove in an attempt to block the wild pitch. His outflung mitt did not reach quite far enough. The ball slanted off the padded outer edge and skittered all the way to the screen outside the Dinner dugout.

Smith scrambled to his feet and chased the ball. Joe hustled in to cover the plate, but the runner from third scored easily. Federal runners from second and first raced around third and second, and another run crossed the plate just as Bill Smith retrieved the ball. The boy from first base reached third.

Joe stood covering the plate, glove extended, but Bill Smith did not throw. "Time!" he called to the umpire, then clumped toward Joe. One shin guard flopped against his leg and knee, jarred loose from a strap buckle in the dive after the wild pitch. Bill fastened the shin guard, straightened and glared at Joe.

"And you're the guy supposed to have got tips from a big leaguer!" Smith spat. His expression mirrored disgust. "Anybody would think this major league pitcher you were buddy-buddy with would have told you about heaving a wild pitch with men on base! That stuff you and your lead-the-cheers-for-Mancin pal put out has to be strictly for the birds!"

"Cool it, Bill!"

The Dinner coach had come from the dugout. He gave his son a stern look and said to the umpire, "Ortega in to pitch for us; he'll bat in Cook's spot. Mancin goes to right field instead of Cook. Bill, get up there and take Ortega's range-finding pitches and knock off side observations!"

Bill Smith sidled near Joe Mancin as the coach turned toward the dugout. "I still say the junk you've put out about Lefty Vroeg coaching you is bunk," the catcher said in low tone.

"I never claimed that Lefty Vroeg coached me," Joe said. "I *did* live next door to Lefty and we *did* work out together."

"Dad said to knock off the side observations." Bill Smith moved faster toward the plate. "And it's a long way out to right field!"

The first batter to face Mike Ortega drove a high fly to left field. Tom Dancer caught the ball a scant yard short of the fence; the runner on third scored after the catch. Then Ortega shut the door on Federal batters. A pop fly to Pete Inglis at shortstop and a strikeout ended the inning. But the 3 that went on the scoreboard for Federal erased the 1-0 lead Dinner had nursed since Joe Mancin's two-base hit scored Harry Tessario in the first inning.

Neither team developed a real scoring threat in the sixth inning. Pete Inglis led off the seventh for Dinner, and singled sharply through the hole between shortstop and third baseman. Pete advanced to second on a short passed ball. The Federal boy on the mound indicated that his battery mate's misplay bothered him. He served two more very poor pitches to Dave Hammer. Pete Inglis got a great jump on the pitcher—who must have been concentrating so much on aiming the ball that he forgot a runner was on base—and stole third. The pitcher threw a second strike to Dave Hammer.

Then the Dinner centerfielder drove the three-and-two pitch on a line over second base, scoring Inglis. Dinner supporters came alive and yelled like crazy when Hammer stole second on the first pitch to Harry Tessario.

Tessario allowed the yells to excite him into being over-anxious and swung at a pitch well above his cap bill. Unfortunately for Tessario, he connected—for a pop-up no more than ten feet behind first base just inside the right field line. Dave Hammer anchored a foot to second base, and bluffed a try for third after the catch, trying to draw a throw. But the first baseman did not fall for the bluff. He carried the ball to the pitcher, arm cocked ready to peg if Hammer did go.

Bill Smith was fooled by a change-up pitch, swung weakly and sent an easy roller that the first baseman fielded a yard in front of the base, paying no attention to Hammer tearing for third. Two out. Score: Federal, 3; Dinner, 2.

Joe Mancin came to the plate. He could not remember a time when he wanted more to get a hit. He stood at the plate, recalling how Bill Smith had scoffed about his not really knowing Lefty Vroeg. And what Lefty had said about Joe's batting came to mind.

You have a good, level swing and you get wrist snap into it that adds to your power. Whether you turn out to be a pitcher, your big bat should earn you a place on your team.

The first pitch was wide; ball one. The pitcher kept the ball away again his second offering. "Ball!" The umpire said. "Two-and-oh!"

Joe remembered some of Lefty Vroeg's advice on pitching. *It's always a battle between pitcher and batter. You try to outguess the batter, catch him not ready. But when you get behind, like a two-and-oh count, you have to watch yourself. You want to get the ball in the strike zone but you have to be careful not to make it too good. The hitter just might not take it, be ready and clobber you!*

Joe gripped his bat tighter; he was ready. The third pitch was a fast ball right down the middle of the plate and just below the letters on Joe's shirt. He brought his bat around smoothly, met the ball on the good wood of the fat part of his bat. There never was a doubt from the instant the sphere shot off the wood. It was high over the right field fence, a home run all the way—a two-run home run.

"I told you! Didn't I tell you that Joe got tips

from a big leaguer?" Carlos Vardez jumped up and down in front of the dugout. "He socks the ball like he pitches—good, huh! That is fact-no-brag—like the TV says!"

Tom Dancer, waiting to bat next, and Joe spatted hands when Joe crossed the plate. Carlos ran out and hugged his husky friend.

Dancer liked the first pitch, swung and lofted an easy fly ball to left field that ended the Dinner seventh—but the figures on the scoreboard were much better—Dinner, 4; Federal, 3.

"Just three little ole outs, Ortega! . . . One, two, three, Mike-kid! . . . Everybody on your toes, gang. The old fight! Dig out the old bench ball and heave it to 'em, Mike!"

His mates chattered fight talk to Mike Ortega as they left the dugout. Ortega tried hard but lost the umpire's decision on a 3-2 pitch and issued free transportation to the leadoff man. The second batter topped a low pitch and dribbled a "swinging bunt" down the third base line. Jim Kubelik came in fast, grabbed the ball and fired to first, but the runner beat the ball by a half-step. Potential tying and winning runs on second and first.

Mike Ortega struck out the third batter.

One out—nothing to worry about, really. The eighth and ninth batters in the Federal hitting order were coming to bat and on deck. Neither had come close to a hit.

"Easy meat, Mike-kid, easy meat up there! . . .

Bust that ole apple past him! . . . The old dark ball, Mike!"

Infielders chattered encouragement. Mike Ortega eyed the base runners and went into his stretch. The pitch was outside and the batter "hit it where it was pitched." A routine fly soared toward right field, an easy catch.

Joe Mancin knew that with less than two outs, runners on first and second normally played outfield fly balls half-way—perhaps not exactly half way to the next base, but certainly not tagging up to try to advance after the catch. He caught the fly no more than a foot inside the foul line, not too deep. Afterward he knew that he hadn't been really alert.

"Watch it!" Lon Alfo yelled. "They're tagged up!"

Momentarily startled, Joe wasted a vital second's fraction to check the second baseman's warning and saw both runners now digging for the next base. He cut loose a hurried peg toward third.

The ball sailed far above Jim Kubelik's head, struck a steel pipe-post supporting the wire screen in front of the stands, and slanted toward the left field corner.

Playing far over toward center field for the left-handed batter who hit the fly, Tom Dancer sprinted after the ball. But he had a long run.

The runner from second tore around third and crossed the plate before Dancer reached the ball.

The runner who had started on first barreled into third and the coach there waved him on. He slid across the plate as Bill Smith waited for the throw.

End of the game. Federal, 5; Dinner, 4.

Bill Smith glowered at Carlos Vardez as Dinner players walked dejectedly from Khoury League Park. "The guy even makes wild pitches from the outfield," Smith growled. "Change that TV fact-no-brag crack to brag-no-fact, and a guy can buy it!"

CHAPTER TWO

There is More Than One Position

CARLOS VARDEZ came at a fast trot up the Mancin driveway. He waved a newspaper clipping excitedly, and Joe shut off the power mower he was guiding around the back yard.

"You see this, Joe?" Carlos asked when the mower noise died. "It was in the morning paper."

"No. You know we don't take the morning paper."

"Yeah." Carlos nodded. "So when I read it I hopped right over here. Read it."

In the lower left corner of the red-bordered clipping, two boys in baseball uniform were depicted. One was a left handed batter standing at the plate, bat ready to swing. Crouched behind him, a boy wearing mask, chest protector and shin guards held mitt and bare hand extended thigh-high to the batter.

Large red letters at the top of the clipping above the batter's head proclaimed: IT'S KHOURY LEAGUE DAY AT BROWARD SHOPPING MALL! Below the red heading smaller black letters announced:

> Broward Mall Wishes to Honor All Khoury League Baseball Players in the Immediate Area. Broward Mall Will Provide Several Prominent Sports Figures as Guests. They Will Mingle with the Boys and Speak Briefly. Each and Every Player Showing up in Our Parking Lot on Saturday Next, in Uniform Between the Hours of 10:00 A.M. and 5:30 P.M. Will Receive ONE HOT DOG AND SOFT DRINK OF HIS CHOICE FREE OF CHARGE. Come! Participate! Help Broward Mall Promote Khoury League Baseball and Good Sportsmanship in Our Community.

Across the bottom of the clipping red letters repeated the time and place—SATURDAY. BROWARD SHOPPING MALL, 10:00 A.M. to 5:30 P.M.

Joe looked up from the clipping. Carlos said eagerly, "Tomorrow morning. We'll go together, huh?"

"No." Joe shook his head. "I told you last night coming home after the game. I'm going to turn in my uniform!"

"But Joe! You didn't mean it! You were just

upset! You were tired and sore at yourself and the world because you had a bad night. You like baseball too much to quit!"

Joe said morosely, "Sure I like baseball. But I can't seem to pitch more than four innings. The team will do better without me! I'm going to quit!"

Carlos Vardez regarded his big friend. "I think not," Carlos said. "I have heard Lefty Vroeg tell you many times that a pitcher has to be able to take rough going. If he quits when batters get to him pretty good, he is dead! You never quit!"

Joe said nothing.

"Besides, there are other places than pitcher to play on a team, Joe."

"Yeah, like outfield! Look what happened when Coach put me in right last night! And another thing, the guys don't go for me; they make fun of me!"

"*One* guy!" Carlos waved his arms. "Why didn't you tell Smith off when he made that crack, I'd like to know!"

Again Joe said nothing.

"You haven't boasted about something not true, you *know* Lefty Vroeg. You afraid somebody'll think you're bragging?"

Carlos waited a moment and when Joe did not answer his question, Carlos shrugged. "Okay," he said, "So I can't argue with a guy who won't say anything. But you'd better do some arguing with yourself. I'll be here Saturday morning before ten o'clock."

Joe was in uniform, waiting for Carlos. He was still not sure whether he was going to turn in his uniform when Coach Smith met the Dinner squad in the usual Monday after-school practice.

He had argued with himself as Carlos advised.

It seemed pretty certain that Joe Mancin on the pitching mound would be more handicap than help to the Dinner team. And making that wild throw from right field had been for sure no help. Still, he had driven in three of the four Dinner runs.

. . . . *your bat should earn you a place on your team. . . .*

He had himself just about convinced that he could really help the Dinners when he thought of the jibes from Bill Smith.

It could be that Carlos was right; maybe he should tell Smith off. But telling people off just was not Joe Mancin's way. He wished that he had some of the assurance Carlos displayed all the time. Nobody would ever suspect that Carlos was not an important cog in the team, just a glorified bat boy. He wore a uniform but was not on the Dinner roster of eligible players. Well, Joe Mancin was not like Carlos and that was that. He sighed as he wheeled his bicycle from the garage.

Carlos came speeding up on his bicycle. "Sorry

to be late," he said. "My mother sent me to the supermarket and the checkout lines were murder!"

"It's not quite ten," Joe said. "Anyway, the thing lasts until five-thirty. I don't think they will run out of dogs or soft drinks!"

"Funny, funny, huh? One of the sports stars is Mendoza Perez. I was a baby and can't remember, of course, but the Perezes and the Vardezes came from Cuba together. Now, Mendoza Perez is making it big in pro football. I wouldn't want to miss him, in case he should be around only a little while."

They rode their bikes to the Broward Shopping Mall parking lot. A section had been roped off and a temporary stand set up that bore a lettered banner fastened to the edge of the canvas top. BROWARD MALL KHOURY LEAGUE HOT DOGS AND SOFT DRINKS.

Scores of boys in baseball uniforms milled about the hot dog stand. Every uniform bore the big block K, a pair of hands gripping a baseball bat and KHOURY lettered above the hands with LEAGUE below, superimposed on the K. This was the official Khoury League emblem.

Joe and Carlos stood their bikes with others near the full bike rack in the Mall parking lot. Carlos looked around eagerly. Suddenly he pointed toward a young man near the hot dog stand and cried, "There he is! There's Mendoza Perez!"

Public address horns installed atop the hot dog

stand blared almost as though Carlos had triggered the announcement: "Attention, boys! We are indeed fortunate to have as a guest an athlete who can give first hand evaluation of youngsters' sports. Mendoza Perez, the microphone belongs to you!"

A tall youth with curly black hair took the microphone and grinned. Except for his height he could have passed for a Khoury Leaguer.

"I never played Khoury League baseball," Perez began. "I played baseball in Cuba, but I was not very good. You could say that I did not try for a Khoury League team when we came to the United States because I knew I was not good enough. But a youngster football league—like Khoury League, only not played with bat and baseball but with goal post and football and—"

Perez stopped and laughed. He said, "I am a naturalized citizen. I have a diploma from a state university. Yet I still make a mess of what I want to say sometimes.

"Kid football gave me a start. I happened to be better than some other kids at catching forward passes. Coaches and players in the kid league taught me a lot; coaches and players in high school and at the university taught me more. You learn all the way up the line.

"I am sure you all know who Lefty Vroeg is. He was a couple of years behind me, but we went to the same high school. He signed a professional baseball contract right after pitching our high school to the state championship. Lefty Vroeg played Khoury League baseball. He really got his start toward a professional career in Khoury League."

Perez lowered the microphone away from his mouth and looked out over the crowd of Khoury Leaguers for a moment, then went on speaking.

"Kid football did a lot for me. I am sure Lefty Vroeg would tell you that Khoury League play did much for him. If any of you have ambition to play professional baseball, I am sure you cannot beat Khoury League training as a start! Thank you."

Joe glanced at Carlos while they both applauded Mendoza Perez. Carlos looked as though he was gazing upon an idol. Joe was about to say something jokingly to Carlos when a commotion in front of the hot dog stand caused everybody to look that way.

"Okay, supposing I did crowd in front of you —so what? I'm the Federal's star pitcher; we're so far ahead that nobody can catch us for the first half championship, and champions should be first. I rate getting my stuff before you do!"

Joe stared at the boy in Federal uniform and saw he was not kidding. He was the one who had yelled derisively from the dugout and had been spoken to by his coach. He *needed* speaking to; you wouldn't think any kid would be like that! Joe took an immediate dislike to the Federal star. Somebody ought to do something about a loud-mouth like him!

Somebody did.

The man behind the counter surveyed the cocky boy, then said, "There's more than one position on a ball club, kid, and they're all important. How about you wait your turn like all the rest?"

"I think you start serving at the other end of the counter, no?"

Mendoza Perez unostentatiously crowded the boy in Federal uniform away from the counter as he spoke to the man behind the counter.

"You are so right, my friend," Perez said. "There are indeed more positions on any team than one—and each is as important as another! You could say, too, that champions should act like *champions!*"

Joe Mancin abruptly felt as though a load pressing down on him had lifted. There *were* other positions on a baseball team besides pitching, and each was important. He knew right then that he would not turn in his uniform, unless Coach Smith asked for it.

CHAPTER THREE

Collision

JOE MANCIN kept looking toward the gate of Khoury League Park. Since Joe had been a member of the Dinner team, Coach Smith had never been late for a practice session, but he was late today.

Well, Coach was Mr. Smith, Science and Math teacher at Broward East High School before he was Walt Smith, coach of the Dinners in the Midget Division of Broward Khoury League. Teachers often had after-school conferences, disciplinary cases or other problems. The thing was, when a fellow wanted to talk over something with his coach he hoped to do it privately before practice began.

"The Old Man finally made it!" Bill Smith observed as the coach came through the gate. "What do you know?"

The Dinner catcher had not spoken loudly, but Joe wondered whether the coach had heard. Walt Smith passed behind his son and said something to him without breaking stride. Bill Smith jerked his head up and looked startled, then a flush colored his throat and cheeks.

"All right, everybody," the coach said. "Sorry to be late. We'll start right off with batting practice and try to make up for the loss of time. Mancin, you take first turn at pitching."

Coach Smith looked toward his son. Joe followed the coach's gaze and noted Bill's sullen, angry expression.

"I'll catch," the coach said. "I didn't bring my mitt, Bill, so you'll have to put up with me using yours. Three cuts each time, twice around the hitting order. Bill and Mike take four turns, then Mike pitch and Bill catch while the rest hit two more turns."

Joe Mancin hesitated. This was no time to bring up what he wanted to discuss with Coach. He caught the ball Walt Smith tossed him, went to the mound—and became sharply aware that Walt Smith wore his son's catching mitt awkwardly on his right hand.

Migosh, Joe thought, *I must have seen Coach throw before. Why hasn't it registered that he is a lefty, too?*

Joe pitched where the coach held his mitt without strain or tension. The ball was rarely more than an inch or two off-target. Why couldn't he pitch like this in a game?

With nothing like baserunners on his mind, or an umpire making calls that seemed always to favor the batter, Joe pondered the question. Well, come right down to it, he did pitch smooth and easy most of the time when starting off a game. It was after four or five innings that he came apart at the seams.

Anyway, why worry about it now? His mind was made up. As soon as he got a chance, he would tell Coach he wanted to give up pitching and concentrate on playing somewhere else.

Bill Smith came to the plate. Even before Joe served a pitch, Bill threw a barb.

"Get that thing in here—if you can! Heave it up and duck!"

Walt Smith straightened behind the plate, raised a hand toward Joe and said, "Hold it!"

He beckoned the boys in the field and the others swinging bats waiting their turns at the plate to gather around him. "Quite apparently a few words are needed before some of you allow wrong ideas to set," the coach said.

He stepped in front of Bill Smith, looked at his son and asked, "Just what was the purpose of yelling at Mancin like that?"

"Why—why—what's such a big deal about razzing a pitcher? Guys in the big leagues—all the professional leagues—do it all the time! Some guys hang on with a club because they're good bench jockeys!"

"You are *not* playing with a professional club," Coach Smith said. "Perhaps professionals stretch things because of pressure to win, win, win, but Khoury Leaguers do not. You all have been indoctrinated in the George Khoury Association of Baseball Leagues *Sportsmanship* Code. No alibis, no unnecessary abusive remarks, no scheming to win at any cost are parts of that code. There will be no more of what you call 'razzing' the pitcher, or any other player. By any of you. Understand?"

His gaze went around the group and came back to Bill Smith. The coach seemed to expect a reply from his son. Bill dropped his eyes and said sullenly, "Yes, sir."

Then he raised his head and burst out, "How come it's always me? At school and now here! Just 'cause I'm your kid, you don't have to—to—well, it's always me that gets landed on!"

Coach Walt Smith eyed his son for a long moment. When he spoke the coach did not raise his voice but there was a steely hardness beneath the soft tone.

"Apparently I haven't landed on you as much as I should have. I intended to discuss this matter privately with you, but perhaps certain things should be impressed on all of you."

He turned to the other boys. "As I indicated to Bill when I came late today, my son is responsible. His homeroom teacher came to me after the teachers' meeting. She hesitated because there has been in her own family an instance of a boy accusing teachers of unfair treatment. There can always be a possibility of delicate situations when a teacher must discipline a child of another teacher."

Joe Mancin wondered if other boys were aware of the change in Walt Smith. He was now very definitely Mr. Smith, teacher, as he stopped momentarily and eyed Bill Smith.

"Causing a disturbance in your homeroom, teasing Carlos Vardez, or whatever you were doing, and then blaming everybody but yourself— including an intimation that you were being 'picked on' because of my being your father—is plain nonsense!"

Walt Smith looked around the group of boys, and added, "Some of you fellows saw and heard Saturday at the Mall what can be the end result of a boy being spoiled. I know his coach spoke sharply to that youngster when he yelled from the dugout the other night; he certainly deserved more than a sharp word after his exhibition at the Mall! He is the nephew of a teacher. He was allowed to get away with mouthing-off until he is now a swell-headed brat, obnoxious to everybody."

The coach held his son's eyes steadily and finished: "It had better be clear to ALL of you that no such actions by *any* member of the Dinner squad will be tolerated! End of lecture. We will practice again tomorrow after school."

The next day Joe rode his bike to the Vardez home. He waited until he and Carlos were pedaling toward Khoury Park, then said, "You got away yesterday pretty fast. What was the thing between you and Smith at school?"

"Nothing to worry about." Carlos smiled and went on so quickly he obviously wanted to change the subject. "It was good to see that you didn't turn in your uniform. I was pretty sure you wouldn't. You just aren't a guy who quits—ever!"

"I hope you're right. What happened that got Smith bawled out by your homeroom teacher?"

Carlos shrugged and said, "He was running his mouth about you and me knowing Lefty Vroeg. I told him it's true that I don't know Lefty like you do, but that Lefty played catch with both of us sometimes. Then Smith shot off his bazoo that you were a big-brag and a nothing-pitcher. I told him what he needed was a punch in the mouth and he said he'd provide the mouth if I wanted to *try* providing the punch. I guess I would have socked him, only that's when the teacher broke it up."

Joe looked at his friend. He almost shuddered at the thought of what stocky, rugged Bill Smith would have done if slender Carlos had punched him. Joe shook his head.

"I wish you—we, that is—had never mentioned Lefty," he said.

Carlos pedaled his bike a half-block in silence. Then he said, "I guess I *have* bragged some. But why does Smith take it out on you? I'd bet he's got a lot to do with you not pitching so hot!"

"That's silly! Bill Smith is a good catcher. If I could always throw where he aims his mitt, maybe I wouldn't come unglued!"

Joe drew in a breath and let it out.

"Maybe any catcher gets sore at a pitcher he believes should not be trying to pitch!" Joe said. "Anyway, today I'm going to ask Coach to let me try for some other position."

Joe wasted no time after they reached Khoury Park. He went straight to the coach, swallowed dryly and blurted:

"I can't pitch! I want to try for some other job!"

Coach Walt Smith studied the boy in silence for what seemed a long time to Joe. He had visions of hearing something like, *"A coach has to be coach. He decides where a fellow can play best and if he doesn't want to do the job there, the only thing is for him to turn in his equipment!"* But Walt Smith said nothing like that.

"You've thought things through, Mancin?" he asked. "All the way?"

"Yes, sir."

The coach nodded. "What position do you have in mind?"

"Any place I can play and help the team."

"There is no rule against anyone playing any position, whether he is right handed or left handed," Coach said. "I think I tried every position when I was a youngster. But the physical handicap of throwing from the wrong side makes it tough for a southpaw to play second base, shortstop, third base or catcher. That leaves outfield and first base, other than pitcher."

"I didn't do the team any good when you sent me to right field!"

"One bad throw doesn't necessarily mean a fellow couldn't play outfield. You caught the fly. As for doing the team any good, let that pass for the moment. Ruling out pitcher and outfield, first base is left."

Coach Smith regarded the big lefthander a moment, then asked, "Do you think you could help us more at first base than Harry Tessario?"

"No, sir!" Joe answered quickly. "Tessario scoops up throws I probably couldn't, and he's a blamed good hitter! I wouldn't want to try first base if it meant shoving Tessario out of the—"

"Excuse me, Coach." The interruption came from a boy with bright auburn hair who came up panting. Red Bennett added, "I'm late because I was at Jim's house when Mrs. Kubelik spilled hot grease on the stove and had to call the fire department. Jim kind of scorched his hand trying to smother the fire. He'll be okay but his mom wanted him to stay home today."

"He should stay home." For a moment Walt Smith seemed to be turning something over in his mind. Abruptly his eyes crinkled at the corners as he looked at Joe.

"An unexpected opportunity for you," the coach said. "I'll do the pitching for both sides and we'll play a three-four inning game with eight men to a team. You take over Kubelik's third base job for our regular starting infield."

Joe Mancin felt all quivery inside when he fielded the final practice hopper that Harry Tessario skipped across the diamond, fired a peg back to the first baseman, and took a position some eight feet from the third base bag. Then as Dick Thomas, left-hand hitting reserve outfielder, stepped into the batter's box, Joe edged farther toward shortstop.

Coach Smith pitched. Dick Thomas swung late and undercut the ball. A pop fly bored high into the air, down the third base line. Joe started in toward the plate. "Mine!" He shouted. "I've got it!"

He heard someone else yell, "Mancin! Mancin's ball!"

The spinning pop-up was not coming as deep as it started. Joe increased his speed, ran all out, never taking his eyes off the ball. He did not see that Bill

Smith was looking up at the ball and tearing from his position behind the plate.

Wham!

Joe and the chunky catcher slammed together and sprawled in a tangle of arms and legs. Joe freed himself, scrambled to his feet and looked around for the ball. Bill Smith writhed on the ground, holding his knee—from which the shinguard had been knocked loose from the strap buckle—and grimacing in pain.

CHAPTER FOUR

But Not This *Position!*

JOE MANCIN sat on the back steps, waiting for Carlos. His Cuban friend had phoned for him to wait before leaving for the extra practice Coach Smith had called. He said that he was bringing something Joe would want to see. Carlos rode up the drive, pushed the stand on his bicycle down and waved the page of a newspaper he carried toward Joe.

"I know you haven't seen the morning paper," Carlos said. "This sheet of the sports section tells about Broward County kid teams."

The first column was headed: Khoury League Player Injury. Joe read the column.

>   Star catcher Bill Smith of the Khoury League
> Dinners, injured in a collision while going after

a pop fly Tuesday, will be lost to his team for at least three weeks.

X-rays and hospital examination disclosed that young Smith suffered a partial ligament tear in his right knee in the collision with Joe Mancin during an intrasquad practice game.

Coach Walt Smith, father of the injured boy, reports that it was 'one of those things,' a collision occuring despite the constant admonition of coaches that players involved in a chase should: 1) yell loudly when they think they have the best shot at catching the ball; 2) back off if a third party yells that the play is so-and-so's.

'Unfortunately,' Coach Smith further stated, 'it can happen that both players yell at the same time and drown out each other, a third party does not yell, or his yell is not heard. Collisions do occur, but coaches and managers from youngster league play to the major leagues feel they should never happen.'

Doctors at City Hospital found no cartilage or internal damage to Smith's knee and surgery will not be required, but the knee will be immobilized in a cast. Coach Smith fears that removal of his catcher for at least three games is surgery already performed on his team's chances to battle Federal for the second half title, and force a playoff for the league championship.

Carlos waited until Joe finished reading the column then said, "Who can Coach Smith get to catch?"

"You've been hoping for a chance to get on the team; why not you?"

"Joe!" Carlos's pained expression nearly matched the anguish in his tone. Then a kind of doubtful thoughtfulness came over his face. "Do you think I dare try?"

"Migosh!" Joe was instantly contrite. "I just wasn't thinking; I forgot. You certainly showed that time you don't lack guts!"

Mentally Joe recalled the first time he and Carlos met. Carlos Vardez and his mother came to live with her parents while a new home was being built for the Vardezes, and the grandparents lived only a few blocks from the Mancin home. Carlos came by while Joe and Lefty Vroeg were working out in the Vroeg-Mancin backyards.

Two pitching distances—one regular 60 feet, 6 inches and one the Khoury League Midget Division 47 feet—were laid out from a piece of plywood Vroeg had sawed to regulation home plate dimensions. Lefty Vroeg was showing Joe how to pitch from the shoulder, eying a make-believe runner on first base right up to the pitching motion.

"It would be better if we had a catcher and you could release the ball," Lefty Vroeg said. Then he spied Carlos standing on the sidewalk at the front of the driveway, watching. "Hey, kid," Vroeg called. "Want to catch for us?"

Carlos nodded eagerly. Vroeg gave him his glove and though it must have felt as awkward as it looked, worn on the wrong hand, Carlos assumed a half-crouch behind the plate and caught Joe's pitches very creditably.

After a while Lefty Vroeg said to Joe, "I'll get my bat from the garage and stand up there like a hitter. It'll give you a more realistic setup to pitch to."

Lefty Vroeg stood at the plate, took several pitches merely holding the bat ready as a batter does awaiting a pitch. Then he swung away above a pitch, and the ball went over the glove Carlos held too low and slammed into his chest.

"Gee, kid," Vroeg said, "I didn't mean to throw you off. I won't swing again."

"No, no!" Carlos protested. "I was watching the bat instead of the ball. I can do it okay."

Lefty Vroeg looked doubtful but finally nodded. Then he swung again, well below Joe's pitch, turned his head and watched.

Carlos did not get his glove near the ball; again it slammed against his chin. Vroeg said, "Like I thought; you blinked your eyes! A catcher can't blink his eyes, kid!"

"No, no!" Carlos protested again. He looked from Lefty Vroeg to Joe and back to Vroeg, blinked his eyes rapidly as though holding back tears and confessed. "I didn't blink; I shut my eyes tight! That bat swishing in front of me scares me to pieces!"

Remembering all this, Joe looked at Carlos and shook his head. "It would be a bad deal for you to try catching," he said. "Coach will probably use someone already certified as a Dinner. Maybe you can get on the team in the position that fellow plays."

"There is a great deal more to catching than merely receiving pitches," Coach Walt Smith said. He looked at Carlos Vardez, Dick Thomas, Hank Strome and Joe Mancin, gathered with him at home plate. "The catcher must be alert every minute when his team is in the field. He must check his team to be sure nobody is out of position. He must study the batters in order to know what pitch to call. He notes the batter's stance and where he takes it in the batter's box.

"Too close to the plate? He may have trouble with pitches well away from him. If a batter stands far back in the box, try him on fast balls coming in high and tight. Does he have a good eye or can he be fooled into going after bad pitches? What kind of pitch did he handle well when he batted before? He shouldn't get another like it. A catcher must think, *think,* THINK!"

The Dinner coach illustrated the stance a catcher should take, a squatting-sitting position to give the sign, then lifting erect to a bent-kneed crouch and holding the mitt as a target where he wants the pitch.

"A catcher must be able to shift his feet, his mitt and his body," Walt Smith went on. "He must be able to change his mitt so the hand points down-

ward to catch low pitches—generally pitches below the waist—and shift the mitt so the hand points upward for high pitches. He must shift right or left for wide pitches to either side of the plate. He must get his body down on his knees to block pitches in the dirt."

The coach went on to explain briefly the art of grabbing the mask off in order to locate pop fouls better, carrying it until the ball is located and then tossing it well out of the way. He illustrated stepping forward with the foot opposite the throwing arm to peg to cut down baserunners and snapping the throw approximately off the ear.

"We cannot possibly cram into you in a couple of days all the things a catcher learns over a long period of time," he said finally. "We are in an unfortunate situation. Every team should have at least one backup catcher, but the position is not one overflowing with appeal to youngsters. So we will have to make do as best we can until Bill recovers."

Coach Smith took Hank Strome first for individual help. While they worked behind the plate, Joe eyed Carlos. "What gives?" Joe asked. "You sure surprise a fellow, trying for catcher after the way you talked!"

Carlos nodded. He was watching the coach showing Strome how to shift his feet. "I think I surprise me, too," he said. "I got to thinking what Mendoza Perez said about how coaches helped him to learn to catch forward passes though he knew nothing about football when he came from Cuba. So, I told myself that perhaps Coach can help me to learn how to catch although I know nothing about it. So, here I am to try!"

Coach Smith worked with Dick Thomas, then with Carlos. Joe was amazed at the quickness Carlos showed in absorbing coaching tips. Walt Smith called Joe last and before he started with the left-hander, Smith produced a left-hand, catching mitt. He chuckled at Joe's surprised expression.

"Like I said, I tried every position when I was a kid." Walt Smith indicated the odd-appearing mitt. "I had to order it special, but I was sure then that I would turn out to be the first southpaw catcher to make the big leagues. You can tell from the almost-like-new condition that my catching ambition never really bloomed. One thing, though, I can show you the movements more naturally than I could show the other boys."

The coach illustrated footwork a catcher must develop in order to shift properly. If the pitch is wide to the right side—place the left foot behind the right and take a wide stride with the right foot. For a pitch wide to the left, place the right foot behind the left and take a wide step with the left.

Foul pops from pitches coming to the plate on the left side are likely to be to the left; pop-ups off pitches to right are likely to be to the left. The experienced catcher turns after foul pop-ups according to the direction of the pitch.

After a while Coach Walt Smith eyed Carlos, Hank, Dick and Joe, and said, "Everything we have covered thus far is pointless unless you have one quality—the ability to stand behind a swinging bat and keep your eyes on the ball.

"Obviously you cannot keep your eyes on the ball if you close them even for the instant of a blink!"

Joe thought of Carlos that first time with Lefty Vroeg. He looked at the slender boy just as Carlos licked his tongue across his lips. Carlos had lost all of his usual cocky assurance.

"As long as you have a protector and shin guards on," Walt Smith said to Joe, "put the mask on and we'll see how you stack up."

A boy with a bat stood in the batter's box while the coach stood off to the side. Smith instructed him to swing but to be sure he did not come close to connecting with the pitches from Mike Ortega.

Joe had no problem. He caught four pitches from Ortega without once blinking. Walt Smith nodded and said to Hank Strome, "Your turn."

"No way!" Strome nodded vigorously. "No way! I'm already lost. I could never learn to shift and jerk off my mask and stuff—and for sure I'd blink!"

Dick Thomas took his place behind the plate. He missed the first pitch, then failed to handle any of the next three cleanly. Coach Smith shook his head sadly.

Carlos Vardez tried only one pitch. The ball went above the mitt he held toward the pitcher and slammed into his chest protector. Carlos took off the mask and mitt, faced the coach and drew in a breath.

"I can't do it," he said mournfully. Then he muttered more than spoke aloud, "If a catcher can't *blink* his eyes; for sure he can't shut them tight! I am sorry Mendoza! As you said, there are many positions—but for me, not *this* one!"

CHAPTER FIVE

Second Half Opening Game

THE DINNER squad sat on the dugout bench; Walt Smith stood facing them. This easy talk between coach and boys before a game was a custom that never varied.

"Westgate is a good team," Smith said, then nodded as though confirming something to himself. His eyes held a sparkle as he went on. "Sure, I know I always begin this way, but believe me, I don't say it just to hear myself talk. Every team in our league IS a good team. And that includes Atom Class, Bantam Class, Midget Class and Junior Class. Go right down the line in our Midget Class setup: Westgate, Northside, Eastgate, Federal and Midway. I would have to be convinced by personally seeing their teams in action before I would admit that any Khoury League Class is better balanced."

One of the boys said, "You left out Dinners, Coach."

"So I did." Walt Smith chuckled. "I wondered if you'd notice—and that leads up to a thing I want to talk with you about. Westgate finished the first half of our season schedule one game behind Federal. Now, every team starts fresh in the standings when we begin second half play, and Westgate has all sights set on finishing on top and earning the right to meet Federal in a playoff for the league championship. Westgate IS a good team, but so are we a good team!"

Coach Smith stopped speaking. His gaze traveled over the boys seated on the bench. An odd thought came to Joe Mancin. It seemed as though the coach expected—was waiting for somebody to say something. After a moment the "something" came from a boy crouched down against the back and side of the dugout at the opposite end of the bench from Joe.

"That newspaper guy's stuff reads kind of like you don't think our prospects are so hot," the boy said. "It reads more like you feel that losing Bill cut our chances to fight Federal for the second half championship clear out."

"Thanks." Walt Smith inclined his head toward Tom Dancer, who seemed to be trying to crowd under the bench. "I hoped one of you would bring up the newspaper piece. And now I hope you will understand that I am not trying to claim that I was misquoted.

"You have to keep in mind that newspaper men only work for their papers. Sometimes they may report quite accurately what you said; I really believe that they try to do so. But when things are omitted, the printed piece comes out entirely different. I have confidence in the man who wrote the column and I accept his explanation that editorial cutting made the thing read as it did."

Walt Smith looked up and down the bench. After a moment he said quietly, "What I told the sportswriter was, quote: Some may say that Bill's removal from the lineup will cut our chances to beat Federal for the second half title. But I do not feel— and I am sure our boys do not feel—that we are dead. We will give the competition a battle, Bill Smith behind the plate or whoever! Unquote.

"We are still the Dinners and we are still as good as any team in our Class. Now, go out and show Westgate that today we are better!"

The leadoff batter for Westgate slapped Mike Ortega's first pitch to Harry Trutt two feet outside the foul line. Then he was fooled by Ortega's change-up pitch and pulled the ball too far. It hopped past third base, eight feet into foul ground.

The batter lofted Ortega's third offering to right field, and Fred Cook moved only two steps to catch the easy fly. One out.

A foul blew back over Joe Mancin's head into the screen. Then a pop-up to Pete Inglis at shortstop sent the second batter back to the dugout. Two out. When the third Westgate boy to come to the plate chopped a one-hopper to Jim Kubelik the third baseman made a fine grab and pegged across the diamond to Tessario for the third out.

Mike Ortega was out of the inning on six pitches—and Joe Mancin had not handled the ball since throwing Ortega's final warmup toss back to the pitcher before anybody came into the batter's box.

"A great job of backstopping!" Walt Smith greeted Joe at the entrance of the screen-enclosed dugout. "Not a semblance of the unsure ballhandling a coach might expect of an inexperienced catcher!"

A twinkle was in Walt Smith's eyes and Joe appreciated the coach's kidding. Smith clapped him on the shoulder and added, "Also, there was nothing left-handed about the job of calling pitches. Nice going!"

Then to his team and particularly to Pete Inglis, the lead-off batter he said: "All right, let's go right now! Make him pitch to you, Pete. Get on base! A big inning could break the game wide open. Let's put one together!"

Pete Inglis worked the pitcher for a walk. When Dave Hammer dumped a "blooper" fly in short right field for a hit that sent Inglis to third, it seemed as though the Dinners just might come up with a big inning that would "break the game wide open."

But Dave Hammer, trying to bother the pitcher by taking a lead as though he was going to steal on the first pitch, led off a little too far. The pitcher's quick snap throw to his first baseman caught Hammer a yard short of the bag, despite his speedy dive back. One out.

Before Bill Smith was hurt, Joe Mancin hit sixth in the batting order, but this day Coach Smith moved him into the third spot. He stood at the plate feeling loose and ready. The first pitch came letter high, seemed outside, but the umpire called, "Strike!"

Joe looked around at him. "It broke across the corner," the official explained.

Joe knew that curve balls were outlawed in Khoury League play up to and including the Midget Division. He did not say anything, but the umpire correctly interpreted his expression as questioning.

"Broke is not the word I should have used," he

said. "This pitcher's fast ball moves as well, maybe better, than yours—only it moves in and out instead of hopping or sinking!"

Joe nodded. Umpires were helpful in Khoury League ball, explaining things impartially. He took another pitch, a change-up-half-speed offering that failed to catch the strike zone. One-and-one. Then a pitch hit the dirt and the catcher went to his knees to block it. Two-and-one. *He'll probably come in there with the fast one,* Joe thought. *Not fat if he can help, but around the plate.*

The pitch was between the letters and shoulders but too far inside. Joe saw the ball start to slant; his reflexes adjusted his swing to the change of pitch as he brought his bat around.

Crack! Then *smack!*

The ball shot off the bat, so hard hit that no Midget League third baseman playing normally could have reached it. But the Westgate hot corner guardian was holding Inglis from taking too big a lead and he was barely away from the bag as the ball ripped down the line so fast that it smacked into the fielder's glove so quickly there seem no elapsed time between *crack* and *smack.*

Perhaps surprised that the ball hit into the pocket of his glove when he instinctively threw it up as protection, the third baseman did not remain surprised. Quickly he took a step and stabbed his foot against the bag. Pete Inglis had no chance and was doubled while still three feet from the base.

The double play ended the Dinner "big inning."

Mike Ortega kept Westgate off the scoreboard in the top of the second, but Joe Mancin did not have an easy inning. The lead-off batter swung at a bad pitch for the third strike, low and outside. Joe knew that unconsciously he relaxed, never thinking the batter would swing. He did not blink but he also did not handle the ball cleanly. He leaped after it when it dribbled from his mitt and his throw to first base was in time to retire the batter.

But that was not good. A catcher had to be alert every second.

He sized up the second batter. A right-handed hitter, he stood well back in the box. Joe recalled Walt Smith's instructions about pitching to such batters. . . . They usually have a good eye and confidence . . . Try them on pitches to the outside of the strike zone. . . . Keep your pitcher moving the ball around. . . . If you follow a pattern, they will be set and ready.

Mike Ortega got a strike on the batter, a fast ball belt high that caught the outside edge of the plate. The Westgate boy refused to fish after two half-speed pitches, one inside and one outside the strike zone. Joe signed for a fast ball along the outer boundary of the strike zone. The instant the ball left Ortega's hand, Joe Mancin knew he had called a wrong pitch.

The batter was set and ready. He stepped into the ball and slammed a drive over the head of secondbaseman Lon Alfo into "power alley" between right fielder and center fielder. The ball took an unexpected hop off the fence and eluded Dave Hammer and the batter raced to third.

Mike Ortega struck out the next batter. Joe almost dropped the third strike, but managed to keep the ball in his mitt. The fourth batter was fooled by the first pitch, swung under the ball and a little late and popped a foul toward first base. Joe grabbed his mask off, and remembered not to throw it until he located the ball.

He relaxed, the pop-up was going deep down the line, Tessario's ball. The first baseman drifted under it, then suddenly threw his arm over his head and ducked. "Take it, Joe!" he yelled. "I've lost it in the lights!"

Joe Mancin learned right then that a catcher is always under a handicap chasing a pop fly or a bad throw because shin guards and chest protector hamper his movements.

He barely managed to get to the ball and to jab his mitt out—luckily soon enough to be under the ball instead of knocking it away. He half-fumbled but managed to slap his bare hand over the ball in time to keep it from dribbling out of the pocket.

"Way to go!" Mike Ortega shouted. "You're a *catcher, Joe!*"

Joe was grateful, but he did not fool himself. "Lady Luck more than smiled on me," he said. "She grinned! It was just plain luck!"

Coach Smith tried to encourage his boys but they went down in order.

Mike Ortega and the Westgate pitcher retired rival batters without run damage again in the third, fourth, fifth and sixth innings. There were no more pop-ups calling for the catcher to field and Joe dropped only one other pitch. It was not a third strike, so caused no damage. The left-handed catcher began to feel confident that he could do the job. Then in the top of the seventh inning, Joe wondered if Lady Luck had wearied of smiling at him.

The leadoff batter flied out to Tom Dancer in left field; the second worked Ortega to three-and-two, then popped up the full count pitch weakly to Lon Alfo.

"Two big ones out of there, Mike! . . . You've got 'em on your hip! . . . Feed this guy the old bench ball! . . . Hold 'em off one more time; we'll get you a run, Mike-kid!"

Infielders aimed pepper-talk at Mike Ortega. Joe raised a clenched fist toward his pitcher and shouted. "Here's the one to get! Pour that apple down the pike!"

Mike "poured" a fast ball "down the pike" and the batter did not offer as the ball split the strike zone. He was completely fooled by another fast ball through the middle of the strike zone, quite evidently looking for a change-up or a waste pitch, and again did not swing. Strike two. Joe signed for a change-up, low and inside.

The batter went for the waste pitch. He swung and did not come within a foot of the ball. But shouts came from the Westgate dugout and from the coaches at first base and third. "Run! Run it out! It's a passed ball!"

Inside and low to the right-handed batter, the pitch was low to Joe Mancin's bare-hand side. He did not get his mitt faced properly and his grab at the ball missed. It was a passed ball, all right—clear back to the screen. The batter raced around first and sped toward second as Joe picked up the ball.

He was wearing Bill Smith's chest protector and the wide part over the left shoulder was designed to protect a right-handed catcher. It cramped the movement of Joe's throwing arm.

His peg to second was high and wide to the left side. It was over the reach of Lon Alfo, covering the bag, and too wide for Pete Inglis, backing up the second baseman. The ball sailed on into left-center-field. By the time Dave Hammer retrieved the wild peg, the Westgate boy was rounding third and the coach waved him on.

Hammer's peg was not the best throw he ever made. Joe failed to block it and the ball skidded past him to the screen.

Westgate had a run without benefit of a hit, walk, flyball or fielder's choice.

Joe Mancin never felt lower.

What was the use?

He had lost ball games for the Dinners when he was pitcher; he had cost them runs and games when he played outfield. Now, he had presented the rival team with a run that was practically one hundred percent gift from Joe Mancin!

CHAPTER SIX

Some Kind of Jinx?

CARLOS VARDEZ stood for a while astride his bike in the Mancin drive before Joe propelled the power-edger around the far end of his mother's back-yard flower border and saw him. Carlos carried the seemingly inevitable newspaper sport section.

Joe shut off the motor. He was eager to read what the sportswriter had written about the opening of the second half Khoury League Midget Class schedule.

"Last week I came; you're mowing. This week I come; you're mowing." Carlos inclined his head toward the machine. "Are you always mowing the lawn?"

"It's just that I mow whenever Dad gives the word." Joe grinned. "This isn't a mower. Dad got weary of Mom sputtering about having to pull grass creeping out into her flower borders. So, he bought this edger, and I get to run it!

"Last week we were off school Friday because of teachers' meeting, so I mowed. Today Dad set up the edging job, so-o-o—What's with you?"

"I told you last night you should not feel bad," Carlos said, "but I know you do. Read what they printed and you'll feel some differently."

Carlos spread the paper so that the headline stood out.

DINNER UPSETS WESTGATE IN SECOND HALF OPENER.

Despite a defense weakened in a vital spot, Coach Walt Smith's Dinner team turned back a confident Westgate squad last night at Khoury Park. The final score of 2–1 accurately reflects the tightness of the game.

Mike Ortega, ace righthander uncovered by Coach Smith, allowed only two hits and walked only one batter: an exceptional pitching accomplishment in any youngster league. Yet it seemed for a time that Ortega's masterpiece would go for naught.

We do not criticize—keep in mind always that these are youngsters under thirteen years of age. But we must report that the Westgate run was not only unearned, it could be put in the category of unbelievable—have a look at what happened.

Joe stopped reading. The vivid mental picture he retained of that nightmare top of the seventh in-

ning was enough. He skipped a couple of para-
graphs, then went on reading.

> Dinners came to bat for the final inning trail-
> ing 1–0. No one could have censured them if they
> had merely gone through the motions. They
> were supposed to be a beaten team.
> Pete Inglis led off and lined out to the left
> fielder. Dave Hammer slashed a wicked grass-
> cutter that the shortstop gloved and pegged
> across to nip Hammer. Two out.
> Harry Tessario fouled off four three-and-two
> pitches and finally walked. Joe Mancin came to
> the plate.
> Laboring under the potential "goat" label
> threat, the big southpaw-pitcher-turned-catcher
> dueled the pitcher to a full count. Then the
> lefthanded hitter pulled a fast ball and rifled a
> hit down the right field line.
> It was not an out-of-the-park home run, but
> it was a drive no more than eighteen inches in
> fair ground when it bounced againt the woven-
> wire fence—and stuck.
> A legitimate two-base hit, perhaps even a
> triple, the solid smash scored Tessario with the
> tying run. The Westgate right fielder played the
> drive to ricochet off the barrier and was forced
> to run thirty or forty feet to pick the ball
> from the fence. Joe Mancin raced around the
> bases and crossed the plate before Westgate could
> get the ball to the catcher.
> Dinners, 2; Westgate, 1
> You can't discount a team that comes through
> after it seemed they were injury-jinxed, so to
> speak.

Joe looked off across the neighbors' back yards
for a moment after finishing the newspaper piece.

Carlos finally said, "Like I told you all the time, you are good for the Dinners no matter where you play!"

"Thanks for bringing the paper," Joe said. "If you don't have anything else to do, stick around. I'll be through before long, for sure in plenty of time to watch the Game of the Week on television. Just might be Lefty Vroeg pitching today."

Carlos grinned. "I was hoping you would want me to stay," he said.

The television screen showed a Detroit Tigers pitcher taking his pre-game warmup. Then the camera swung across the diamond in Tiger Stadium and showed a tall left-handed pitcher in the blue-gray uniform of the visiting team, also warming up.

"It's him!" Carlos cried. "That's Lefty Vroeg! Right?"

"For sure," Joe agreed. The southpaw pitcher on the screen completed a pitch and his follow-through carried his body around so the numerals on his back were visible. "Number 49," Joe said. "Lefty figured it was a good omen when he got the same number he wore in high school and Legion ball. But you could tell that's Lefty, anyway. He looks skinny as always."

Lefty Vroeg's team failed to score in the top of the first inning, but they failed by a narrow margin. Two men were left on base when the long-ball slug-

ger rifled a drive into the stands that was no more than two inches outside the foul marker, then flied to left for the third out.

The rookie southpaw struggled through a first inning that must have been frustrating to the Tigers—four solid smashes off his delivery, and three of them straight at fielders.

"He doesn't look so hot," Carlos said.

"He got 'em out." Joe nodded. "Don't forget that these are major league hitters, not high school batters. It would have been better for Lefty, maybe, if he'd got more experience before they brought him up to—hold it!"

Joe held up a hand to silence Carlos when the voice of the television sportscaster observed in his between-innings tone. ". . . . and young Vroeg recalls to this announcer a great left-handed pitcher named Koufax. Sandy Koufax pitched no-hitters and many, many low-hit games for the Los Angeles Dodgers when he appeared so thin that one marvelled he could stand the grueling grind of major league pitching. Batters who faced his blazing speed and assortment of stuff never thought of Sandy Koufax as frail. We would say that batters who face young Vroeg also waste no sympathy on his seeming fragility! Actually, Vroeg weighs in at 187. Since it is carried on a six-foot-three frame, this weight may increase. Vroeg is only nineteen!"

The game went on, a scoreless pitcher's duel

until Lefty Vroeg's team gave him a one-run lead in the top of the eighth inning.

"Now," the television voice said as Vroeg completed his range-finding pitches and faced the lead-off batter, "comes the crux of the situation for Rookie Lefty Vroeg. He has pitched brilliantly at times since being brought up to the parent club; too soon, many knowledgeable men believe. Vroeg's difficulties have come from inability to survive late-inning assaults."

Lefty Vroeg did not survive the Detroit attack in the bottom of the eighth.

A walk, a solid smash through the infield, a topped dribbler down the first base line put runners on third and second and one out. Vroeg's manager ordered an intentional walk to fill the bases and set up a possible double play.

Whether it was the walk, or whatever, Vroeg lost all semblance of being a major league pitcher. He hit the batter to force the tying run across the plate. Then four straight bad pitches walked in a second run, and a sharp single scored two more. That was it for Lefty Vroeg.

The sportscaster filled in detail after a relief pitcher came from the bullpen to replace the rookie southpaw.

"No one really expects today to mark the swan song appearance of Vroeg as a major league pitcher, but it could be. We have permission from Vroeg's manager, pitching coach and the club's front office to break the news that Vroeg had to deliver in this game or else.

"The 'or else' means only that Vroeg is being sent down to a farm club. Quote from the pitching coach: 'The boy's confidence has drained away. We do not want to make Vroeg into a reliever and we cannot afford to use him as a starter until he regains confidence. He would never do it sitting on the bench. Vroeg has great potential and we are not giving up on him. Our farm club manager in Florida has worked quirks out of young pitchers before; we are sure that he and the boy can work out whatever causes Vroeg to fall apart in late innings.' Unquote."

A commercial message appeared on the screen and when the ball game came back on, nothing more was said about Lefty Vroeg.

"They can't do this to Lefty!" Carlos Vardez said, then doubtfully, "Can they, Joe?"

Joe Mancin did not consciously hear Carlos. He was frowning at the television screen as though stunned. Words the sportscaster said ran through his mind. *Inability to survive late-inning assaults.*

They could just as well be said about Joe Mancin.

Lefty Vroeg had been an outstanding pitcher in high school. He pitched his team into the final of the State High School Baseball Tournament his senior year. He signed a pro contract the day after throwing a one-hit shut-out to win the state championship title.

Joe Mancin owned the best won-lost and earned-run record of all the pitchers in the county Khoury League Bantam Class last year. Was there something about left-handed pitchers that caused them to run into late-inning difficulties when they moved up to a league of higher classification?

Was there some kind of jinx riding Joe Mancin and Lefty Vroeg?

CHAPTER SEVEN

Two Games—One Rained Out

COACH WALT SMITH faced his team in the dugout before the Dinner-Midway game. He waited for quiet.

"Surprise tonight," he said. "I'm not going to tell you that Midway will be tough—I'm going to tell you they will be *tougher!* Midway finished in last place the first half and we beat them badly both games we played. They lost to Federal in their second half opener. So, why do I say they will be tougher?"

The Dinner coach swept his gaze along the dugout bench.

"I will name no names," he said after a moment. "The guilty fellows know—it could be that all of you are guilty, but I overheard only three.

'They couldn't beat a carpet! . . . We knocked them off twice already and they have the same guys! . . . We can coast tonight and practice up for Northside next week! . . .' Overconfidence has beaten more teams than you can count!"

Walt Smith paced several steps in front of the Dinner team.

"Think about this," he said after a time. "Midway lost a dozen boys from a squad that finished a strong third last year. But the twelve boys that came up to them from Bantam Class play now have eleven Midget League games under their belts. They are no longer Bantam League players, perhaps a little unsure of themselves. Federal had to come from behind last week to edge them 12-11. You had better believe that they score runs and they will be tough!"

Joe Mancin crouched behind the plate to take the range-finding tosses from Forest Ennis, the pitcher Coach Smith had designated to start for the Dinners. He thought, *what Coach didn't say about Midway being tough, is that they won't be facing Mike Ortega and that Ennis got clobbered more often than not when he pitched in the Bantam League.*

He held his mitt to present a target that would be about belt high to the average Midget Leaguer. But Forest Ennis threw the ball so high that Joe had to leap to catch it. Joe said nothing, merely shook his head when he threw the ball back to the pitcher.

The second pitch was almost as high as the first.

"Get 'em down," Joe called. "Take it easy!"

Ennis threw three more pitches, all high. Joe pegged down to Lon Alfo at second, trotted halfway to the pitcher's mound and said, "Just whip that apple up there at my mitt, Ennis. Zero in on the target!"

For a moment he wondered why the words sounded familiar. Then he knew that he was repeating favorite cries of Bill Smith to a pitcher. The cast would be taken off Bill's knee any day, now. Another week and the chunky catcher would be taking over the backstopping chores—and man, would that be a relief!

But right now it was up to a left-handed catcher named Mancin to do what he could to steer his pitcher over whatever roughness came up.

The roughness was lack of control.

Forest Ennis was a long-armed, tall boy. He seemed unable to throw the ball lower than his own shoulders. He delivered three poor pitches—all high—then aimed carefully and got the umpire's call on a borderline pitch at the top of the strike zone.

"Way to zing it in there!" Joe Mancin yelled. "Now you've got the range!"

The next pitch was higher than any of the first three.

Ennis failed to hit the strike zone at all for the second batter. Joe called time, and went out to the mound. He knew how Ennis felt.

"Sometimes a fellow starts out kind of wild," he said, "but you can't let it get you down. Forget those guys on base. Heave that apple up there where I hold the mitt. You can do it!"

Joe crouched behind the plate and held his mitt as low as he could without facing it down. But an instant after the ball left the pitcher's hand, Joe straightened and leaped high to his right. The pitch was so wild he could not reach it. The ball whammed against the screen behind home and base runners advanced to third and second.

Coach Smith stood at the entrance end of the dugout when Joe looked toward him. The coach signaled for time and came to talk to Ennis. Smith did not ask Joe anything.

"You're pressing," Walt Smith told Ennis. "You're tight as a drum; loosen up. I know you can do better than you are showing. Seven boys out here behind you will help but they can't do anything when you walk batters. Get the ball over the plate. Make 'em hit to get on!"

Ennis seemed to have profited from the coach's advice. He threw two good strikes to the next batter. Then Joe called for a change-up, holding his mitt outside the plate. The ball did not come in outside. It was a little high but so near the strike zone that the batter could not risk taking it and being called out on strikes. He swung and hit a ground ball to Alfo.

Usually dependable, the second baseman hurried too much this time in his eagerness to start a double play. His throw was wide past Pete Inglis. The runner coming into second tore for third. Tom Dancer came in fast and grabbed the ball— then pegged so wide to third that Jim Kubelik was drawn five feet off the base.

The batter had reached first and when Dancer threw to third, ran for second. Kubelik's throw to the midway base was perfect, right on the bag, but neither Inglis nor Alfo covered the base. The ball sailed on into right field; the Midway boy scooted to third.

Three runs scored, nobody out, on what should have been a double play, or certainly one out. Fred Cook retrieved the ball and threw it in to the second baseman. The tall pitcher walked around the mound, kicking at the dirt. Joe signaled the umpire for time and went out to the mound. He knew how a pitcher felt when fielding lapses of teammates allowed runs to score.

"No pitcher can help but be bugged when guys boot in runs," he told Ennis. "Okay, so you should have got by with only one run—maybe none if Lon made the play to me. It's all part of being pitcher. It's not your fault."

"What do you mean, not my fault? I loaded the bases with walks!" Ennis wailed. "I just don't have what it takes! I didn't have it last year and—"

"An attitude like that will get nobody anywhere!" The interruption came from Walt Smith. The coach had come from the dugout without Joe or Forest Ennis being aware of him. "For sure," Smith went on, "you won't have it if you don't believe in yourself!"

"Take me out!" Forest Ennis almost sobbed. "I —I—well, maybe I never *will* have what it takes to pitch!"

Walt Smith eyed the tall youngster a long moment. "Desire," the coach finally said, and Joe Mancin got the odd impression that Walt Smith was talking to him as much as Ennis. "Desire," Smith repeated. "You can be endowed by nature with the requisite tools, but if there isn't the old desire— well, okay, Ennis!"

He turned toward the Dinner bullpen and motioned a pitcher to come in.

Paul Orton was another boy who had pitched against Joe Mancin in Bantam Class ball the previous year. A birthday just two days late carried Orton out of the "under eleven" limit of Bantam Class this year.

More than "somewhat on the thin side," Paul Orton was a boy who was late in physical development. Large hands and large feet were signs that one day he would be big. But right now he did not appear to have the physical stamina to take "under thirteen" Midget League competition.

However, Orton started out as though he owned all the batters. In contrast to Ennis, when the fragile-appearing Orton threw the ball outside the strike zone, it was intentional or awfully, awfully close to a strategic pitch.

He retired Midway without further scoring.

It took Dinner three innings to overcome the 3-0 lead Midway notched off Ennis. Then in the top of the fourth Paul Orton gave the first evidence that his strength was being over-taxed. Midway scored two runs on solid hitting after two out. Score: Midway, 5; Dinner, 4.

"How do you feel?" Walt Smith asked Orton in the dugout.

Paul Orton took off his cap and wiped his sleeve over sweat-dampened blond hair. "Tired," he admitted. Then he added hastily, "But I can get 'em out, Coach. Don't worry!"

Walt Smith nodded. Joe Mancin hoped that they could score enough runs to give Orton a cushion. Paul Orton had desire, and guts, for sure.

Dinner hitters chased the Midway pitcher off the mound that inning. They combined four hits, two walks, a fielder's choice and a throwing error and chalked up a half dozen runs that seemed to put the game on ice. The scoreboard showed Dinner,

10; Midway, 5 as Orton finished his range-finding tosses before starting the fifth inning.

Then the roof fell in.

Joe Mancin knew that Orton was struggling when he lost the lead-off batter after having him in a 1-2 hole. The next Midway boy at the plate crossed up everybody. Who would expect a bunt when his team was five runs down? It was a fine bunt, stayed fair just inside the third base line while Jim Kubelik hovered over it, hoping it would roll foul. Two on base, nobody out.

The next batter drove a change-up pitch safely to right-center.

One run in, runners on first and third; Joe called time and went out to the mound. Beads of sweat covered Orton's forehead, but he grinned and muttered, "I'll get 'em out!"

When Orton missed the strike zone by eight inches on a full count and walked the bases full, Joe looked toward the dugout. Walt Smith inclined his head, raised a hand toward the bullpen and two pitchers out there began throwing harder.

Orton battled the next hitter but he was tiring rapidly. In his own words later, he was "all pooped out." The batter met a three-and-two pitch squarely on the good wood of his bat. His lusty drive rocketed off the center-field fence, chased three runs across the plate and left him perched on third.

Mike Ortega came in to relieve Orton and

struck out a batter, forced the second to pop to Jim Kubelik and left the potential tying run still on third with another strikeout. Ortega was as effective in the sixth and seventh innings. At the end of the game scoreboard figures still registered a 10-9 win for Dinner.

As they discussed the game while riding their bikes home, Carlos Vardez and Joe Mancin agreed that when Mike Ortega was not pitching, Dinner was in trouble. "What we need," Carlos said, "is for you to get back to pitching, Joe!"

The schedule set it down as Dinner versus Northside. But as teams finished pre-game workouts, it became more Weather-permitting versus Rainout. South Florida weather is always unpredictable as to rain. It can be clear and fair one minute, and then a squall line, a quirk in high or low pressure systems or a change in cold fronts or warm fronts can bring rain in torrents the next.

This night it was a combination of several weather conditions.

Mike Ortega started on the mound for Dinner and retired Northside one-two-three. Northside's ace pitcher, a veteran left-hander in his final year of Midget League ball, proved to be as tough on Dinner hitters as Ortega had been on his opponents.

The pitchers matched performances in the second inning, repeated in the third. Ortega sent three

Northside batters back to the bench in the top of the fourth—then came the rain.

Rain, more rain, then so much rain that all spectators disappeared and players huddling beneath inadequate dugout roofs became thoroughly soaked. Umpires called the game.

Nothing to nothing, the game would have to be replayed.

Joe Mancin could not get a thought out of his mind. If the rain continued a while, games would pile up to be played later. Ellis and Orton had shown that they could not carry the load to support Mike Ortega. Even this one rained-out game could ruin Dinner.

He was thankful that Bill Smith would be able to take over the catching duties next game—but for sure, the future did not loom too bright for Dinner, with only one dependable pitcher.

CHAPTER EIGHT

Television Appearance

THE NOTE was fastened to the door handle of the refrigerator when Joe came home after school Tuesday. He grinned. Mom knew he would be at the fridge the first thing for something edible and a glass of milk. He read the note.

> Joe: You are to phone Coach Smith when you get home. I've talked with your father and you have our permission to go. Okay to demolish the remainder of Sunday's roast, but don't dig into the pot of Swiss steak. Don't leave a mess.

Joe crammed a sizeable hunk of roast beef into his mouth, made a huge sandwich that consisted of more meat than bread, and poured a glass of milk. Then he lifted the phone off the wall and dialed the number of Walt Smith.

He wondered idly why Coach wanted him to phone? An announcement over the intercom at school stated there would be no practice today at Khoury Park diamonds, still wet from downpours over the weekend. Maybe Coach had found some other diamond dry enough for practice. For sure he wanted some Dinner practice time before Bill Smith went into a game this week.

But that was kind of 'way out thinking. Mom's note would have said something about it, if a practice was—and what about Mom's and Dad's "permission to go?"

"Hello." The voice that came over the line was a surprise. For a moment Joe thought he must have dialed a wrong number. A woman's voice said again, "Hello?"

"Mr. Walter Smith's residence?" Joe asked hesitantly.

"This is Mrs. Smith. Walter has been called to the television studio. Are you Joe Mancin?"

"Yes, ma'am."

"Good. Walter instructed me to tell you to be ready, that he will pick you up no later than 4:30. He talked with your mother, I believe?"

"Yes, ma'am. She left a note. Could you tell me where we are going?"

"To a ball game in Miami!"

Joe was surprised to see that Walt Smith was alone when the coach pulled his car into the Mancin driveway. Walt Smith said, "I didn't intend this to be a production, Joe. I explained to your mother. Jack Murphy, WBCE-TV sports director, asked me to get hold of you and brief you on the situation. Joe, you and I are going to appear on TV—with Lefty Vroeg!"

Joe stared wide-eyed at the Dinner coach. Walt Smith chuckled, then said, "Actually, you have more to do with the whole business than I have. I don't believe Lefty Vroeg would have gone for it, if you weren't involved."

Joe waited until the coach backed from the drive and straightened into the quiet all-but-deserted residential street. Then he said, "I know the farm club they sent Lefty to plays Miami tonight and tomorrow. But what's this about Lefty and us being on television?"

"We'll be on I-95 soon," Walt Smith said, "and talking is no good for anyone driving in expressway traffic. Listen closely now, and when we get on the expressway just consider things and ask any questions later."

He slowed the car a little.

"I've had a theory all along about Lefty Vroeg's late inning difficulties," Smith said. "It ties in with my belief about high school games being reduced to seven innings. Baseball started out to be a nine inning game and still is in professional games. I believe that Lefty Vroeg is a victim of the seven inning high school program. Why it did not occur to me that your difficulty in pitching past the fifth inning could be about the same as Vroeg's, I just don't know."

Joe frowned. What the heck did that have to do with being on television?

"During the past three weeks I've watched four games played by the Bantam Class team you pitched for last year," Smith said. "I always look at as many Bantam Class teams as I can because I want to see what players to go after when they grow out of Bantam Class age. Then something in the back of my mind kept nagging at me as to why I watched your old team so often."

Walt Smith broke off while he negotiated a four-way stop intersection, then went on talking.

"Section 9 of Rule 9, Official Khoury League Rules. Quote: Every boy shall play a minimum of three full innings and have one time at bat in every 6½ or 7 inning game, provided the boy is present at the regularly scheduled starting time. Penalty: Game forfeited. Unquote. Did your Bantam team ever forfeit a game under that rule, Joe?"

"No, sir."

"Nor did any team I ever coached." Smith nodded. "I don't believe many such forfeits occur. Now, I was impressed with a rather peculiar thing while watching your old Bantam team. Your coach made substitutions after four innings—right?"

"Yes, sir."

"Did you ever pitch more than four innings for him, Joe?"

"No, sir. There were two other pitchers. In every game the starting pitcher would be taken out and either put on the bench or sent to the outfield or something. We sort of took turns."

"Your coach misinterpreted the rule," Smith said. "It does *not* require a pitcher to be substituted after 4 innings."

He turned the car onto the ramp that led to busy I-95.

"You and Lefty Vroeg were victimized because you did not pitch beyond a fixed number of innings. The only restriction on the innings a boy may pitch in Khoury League ball is stated in Section 10 of Rule 9: no boy may pitch more than 10 innings in any seven consecutive day period during the regular season, etc."

Joe said, "But how was Lefty victimized?"

"I don't think there is any limitation as to the number of innings a boy may pitch in high school. No, I know there isn't. Some youngster pitched twenty-four innings for a Hialeah high school team in 1970. But Lefty Vroeg still had a seven-inning complex when he went into pro ball, I believe. It had to be cured. I think his manager down here has done it. I believe we can cure your trouble as well —now consider things and ask questions later, if you want."

Walt Smith turned the car into the stream of traffic on I-95.

Joe Mancin had never before been in Miami Stadium. He also had never been closer to a professional baseball stadium than shots of major league ballparks shown during televised games. Joe had read a piece in a Miami newspaper not long before that claimed Miami Stadium was as fine as any minor league city owned, and a lot better than most. To Joe's awed view the claim seemed more than justified.

When an usher showed them to the field box beside the visiting team's dugout, Joe looked wide-eyed at Coach Smith. "Courtesy of Lefty Vroeg," Smith said. "He left complimentary tickets for us at the box office. He'll probably come over when he sees you're here."

The visiting club was taking pre-game practice, infielders grabbing grounders batted to them by a gray-haired man at the plate and zinging the ball to different bases according to his call. Players scattered across deep left-centerfield were running after —and usually catching—fungo fly balls and long drives.

Joe had eyes only for pitchers throwing to two catchers in the bullpen. One of the two lefthanders throwing was taller than the other, and when his follow-through carried his body around after a delivery, Joe saw the 49 on the back of his uniform shirt.

"Hey, Lefty! Lefty Vroeg!" Joe leaped to his feet and waved wildly toward the bullpen before he thought. Then he realized that he was not yelling across the Vroeg-Mancin backyards and sat down abruptly. "Gosh," he muttered. "I hope he didn't hear me!"

But Lefty Vroeg had heard. He said something to an older man in the gray-blue uniform of the visitors who stood watching the pitchers and the coach looked toward the seats beside the dugout and nodded.

Lefty picked up a warmup jacket and put it on while he trotted toward the field box. He was almost there when a man came from the dugout and took his arm. A shield on the man's jacket was lettered WBCE-TV.

"That's Jack Murphy," Walt Smith said. "He told me that everything was all set with Vroeg, but from the way Lefty looks there could be a foul-up."

"Okay, so I agreed to an interview." Lefty Vroeg's words were audible to Joe and Walt Smith. "It's still okay, but it will have to be short, and pretty darn soon. Things have changed since we talked over the phone."

"Whatever you say." Jack Murphy shrugged. "Believe it or not, Walt Smith and the youngster will draw more attention from our local viewers than—hey, what am I saying? For the moment I forgot that you are a graduate of Broward Khoury Leagues."

"If your camera and recording equipment is set up, let's go," Lefty Vroeg said. "You'll have to get everything you want here; there can't be any studio visit for changes or anything. In just over an hour I'll be on a plane, so there is no time to waste."

"Right." The television man made a little gesture and disappeared into the dugout. Lefty Vroeg came to the field box, grinning widely.

"Joe Mancin," he said, "in person! It's really great to see you, kid!" The ballplayer inclined his head to Walt Smith. "Ditto to you, Coach. I see you picked up the tickets."

Then Vroeg grinned and shook his head. "Here I'm trying to get rid of high school habits," he said, "then pull an observation about second grade caliber like that!"

Walt Smith said, "You're looking fit."

"Are you going to pitch tonight?" Joe asked.

"Well, it's my turn and I was scheduled to start, kid. But there has been a change." Then Vroeg said to Walt Smith, "You wrote me that you thought I could help Joe over the hump with a thing he has. What's the problem?"

"Very similar to yours, I think. This plane you will be on in an hour—you're rejoining the big team?"

"Blink just told me when I asked permission to

come in for this television thing." Lefty Vroeg nodded. "The telegram ordering me to report tomorrow in Chicago was delivered only a few minutes ago. If it wasn't that I promised this interview, I would be in the clubhouse now, changing clothes."

"Then your problem must be solved."

"Blink had it figured right off," Vroeg answered. "He's our pitching coach down here. He asked me the very first night whether I'd ever pitched more than seven innings before I went pro. I hadn't. You know, this high school seven inning business does nothing for a pitcher who goes professional!"

"I've always contended that high school games should be nine innings." Smith agreed. "What did Blink do to cure you?"

"He gave me plenty of work, for one thing. He had me pitching every night, either starting a game, working in the bullpen, or in there bailing out some other chucker in trouble. It got so I didn't know what inning I was pitching.

"But the best of Blink's therapy for ailing pitchers—me, anyway—was hammering into me over and over the fact that desire and concentration have to be big with a pitcher. Bad breaks, poor umpire calls, errors—whatever—the pitcher has to put everything else out of his mind and concentrate on battling the batter up at the plate *now!* One game went into extra innings without my really being conscious of it, and a couple of errors put guys on first and third and nobody out. A run was going to ruin us. It was that night that Lefty Vroeg sort of came of age as a pitcher! I battled every hitter coming up that inning—and they did not score!"

"And you feel that you have licked your problem," Smith said.

"Blink made me see it was a psychological block." Lefty Vroeg nodded. "And that game convinced me I could keep on pitching for any given time. I'll take my lumps—no pitcher can escape being pounded around once in a while. But hitters won't get me out of there because it is the eighth inning, ninth, tenth or whatever!"

Jack Murphy appeared before Vroeg and said, "We're all set. Down here in front of the dugout."

Joe did not have time to be awed by practically being in a professional team's dugout. The TV man reeled off an introduction, ending with: "We have just learned that Lefty Vroeg is on his way back to the big league," and shoved the microphone near the ballplayer.

"Right." Lefty nodded. "And this time things are different. There is no doubt that I reached the big time too soon. The jump from facing high school batters to working on big league hitters is awful big. Also, I was cocky because things had come so easy. The club needed left-handed pitching and I was called up before I had my feet on the ground even with the farm club I'd been sent to. So, I fell flat on my face!

"Hitters began rapping my stuff in the eighth inning. Maybe I subconsciously let up after seven innings, like I had pitched in high school. Anyway, I couldn't get anybody out after seven or eight innings right along, and I lost my confidence. Now, the big club is desperate for southpaw pitching again and I'm getting another chance. If desire and work and humility and more work count, this time I'll stay up there!"

The television interviewer stuck the microphone in front of Walt Smith. He made a statement that was entirely in error, perhaps misled because he had heard Vroeg call Smith "Coach."

"Coach," he said, "you had Vroeg in Khoury League ball. He was an outstanding pitcher, as he was later in high school, but certainly coaching contributed to Vroeg's development. What would you say is most important to a youngster with ambition to pitch?"

Walt Smith made no correction and answered the question directly. "Desire," he said. "Lefty put his finger on the greatest asset a pitcher can have. Without desire, natural abilities and talents can be wasted. You have to *want* to be a pitcher!"

"Fine, Coach." Jack Murphy switched the microphone to Joe. "Here is another southpaw being developed in Khoury League ball," the interviewer said. "Joe Mancin stood rival batters on their ears in Bantam Class ball—but we understand that Joe ran into trouble similar to Lefty Vroeg's when he moved up to Midget Class. Right, Joe?"

Joe Mancin never had felt more stupidly helpless. He could not take his eyes off the mike in front of his face and his vocal apparatus seemed as paralyzed as if a line drive had smashed against his Adam's apple. He nodded dumbly.

"But Coach Smith tells me that your team needs you. They have only one reliable pitcher now —two would practically guarantee a championship. You can be the second reliable pitcher. Right, Joe?"

This time Joe could not even nod. He wished he was anywhere but here with that overpowering monster of a microphone stabbing at him.

"Do *you* have desire, Joe?"

Desperation was in the television man's tone. Joe learned later that Jack Murphy's misery at being unable to pull a response from him was as great as his own discomfort.

"And when you come back with the old desire to pitch your team to glorious victory—whoa, Jack!" The WCBE-TV shield on his jacket seemed to droop with his shoulders and his laugh sounded hollow. "Don't get carried away! How about it, Joe?"

Joe Mancin shifted his weight from one foot to

the other, ran his tongue across dry lips and looked appealingly at Lefty Vroeg.

"He'll win it for Coach Smith," Lefty said. "I guarantee my warmup buddy will come back for the Dinners—and win the whole ball of wax!"

CHAPTER NINE

At the Supermarket

WALT SMITH increased his car's speed as he swung it off the entrance ramp into the merging traffic lane of the expressway. He checked the first route marker he saw and said:

"Looks as though I made it right we're on I-95 North okay. I've learned that when I drive in Miami I'd better check whether I'm going the right way. Once I missed a sign coming from International Airport, and drove across Biscayne Bay into Miami Beach before there was a place to get off the expressway and turn back.

"I enjoyed the ball game, but I am well satisfied to have the television business over and be headed home."

"Boy, me, too!"

Smith chuckled. "You really froze, and I wasn't much better. That mike scared me, too—and I'm used to talking. But even though I saw you were in a bad way and Jack's show was falling apart, my mind went absolutely blank. It was good that Vroeg came on and took us off the hook. He certainly saved things for Jack."

Joe said nothing. They rode quite a way; then the Dinner coach said, "Vroeg made a rather broad 'guarantee', which I hope comes off a hundred per-cent. I'm just as sure you can win for us as he was. I think you will lick the—well, our school psycholo-gist talks about mental blocks and such.

"You and Vroeg suffered very much the same, whatever you call it. His manager helped Lefty over the hump and maybe I can help you. You're going to have the opportunity—taking for granted that you *want* to pitch."

"Yes, sir. I want to pitch." Joe's tone could not have been more earnest. "I don't think I ever really *didn't* want to pitch! It was guys saying things like I was a false alarm and making cracks about me not really knowing Lefty Vroeg and—"

Joe broke off. He suddenly remembered that Bill Smith was the "guys" who made the cracks. Again they rode an appreciable distance in silence. When he did speak, Walt Smith seemed to be talk-ing mostly to himself.

"A man deals with young people in his work,

and even younger boys in coaching Khoury League," he said. "Still he sometimes forgets that each one is an individual and just may not fit into some mold he has conceived."

Smith slid a brief glance at Joe, swiveled his eyes back to the highway, and said, "All right, maybe just talking will help—you as well as a fellow named Walter Smith. Let's consider Bill's needling you. I talked with our school psychologist about Bill suddenly using slang and poor grammar as though he were deliberately baiting me. Apparently that, and other problems in our relationship, is basically as much me as it is Bill. The same is true of Bill's bristling and jabbing at you—partly, at least, my fault!"

Joe looked quickly at the coach. He started to say that Smith must be putting him on but changed his wording to: "You—you're—you have to be kidding!"

"No." Smith shook his head. "I thought I was being kidded, too. But when he explained and I added things up, it made some sense.

"You and I are left-handed. Bill tried to be left-handed when he began to throw a ball, but he is NOT left-handed and I never tried to make him left-handed. However, he apparently acquired a fixation that I wanted him to be like me.

"Now, you come to the Dinner team and you're left-handed and you're good. Believe me, I have done more than a little soul-searching since the psychologist advanced his theory. Certainly I never consciously favored you but I can see that Bill may have thought I did. Perhaps there is a kind of unconscious brotherhood of southpaws!"

Walt Smith frowned as though he might be wondering. Then he continued. "Now, consider your telling me you weren't going to pitch anymore: I was sure that you didn't mean it. I don't know whether I handled you poorly. There is this thing about desire that was implanted in my thinking by a coach I had years ago. I believe that desire is a big factor in any athlete's success. I would never back down from that belief."

Again the man gave Joe a brief glance.

"So, consider Coach Smith," the man said. "It well could be that sometimes he overlooks the fact that coaching a Midget Class team in the Khoury League is far from the same as coaching or managing a pro club. I suppose I said to myself something like   let-him-have-his-head-till-he-comes-begging-to-pitch-he-has-to-want-to-do-it. In all probability I would have been after you to pitch again—but things sort of got out of control."

Walt Smith abruptly laughed aloud and shook his head from side to side.

"If it didn't appear that things are going to come around okay," he said, "I would ask our psychologist to analyze me! In any case, I'm happy that you want to get out there on the pitching rubber again. And I am going to work you the way Vroeg's manager worked him, starting with the practice I hope we can get in tomorrow after school!"

Rain came again Wednesday morning and continued until mid-afternoon. There could be no practice for anybody at Khoury Park. Joe asked Carlos Vardez to come after school and catch for him in the backyard "bullpen" he and Lefty Vroeg had used.

"Sure." Carlos grinned. "That's if it is understood there will be no batter like the other time!"

"No batter. It's just that if I'm going to pitch again, I need to be working my arm into pitching shape."

"I knew you would pitch again." Carlos nodded. "You'll win games for the Dinners, too."

"I hope so."

"I'll be at your place after school as soon as I can," Carlos said.

Joe wondered what "soon" meant to Carlos while he waited that afternoon. Finally Carlos slid his bike to a stop in the driveway.

"Supermarket!" Carlos shook his head. "I don't think my mom ever remembered all she needed while she was at the supermarket. Always she has to send me back for something she did not get!"

His tone was more resigned than bitter.

"I go there so often everybody at the supermarket knows me!" Carlos said. "I don't think their day would be complete if I didn't show up!"

Joe threw easily at first, then increased his speed until after ten minutes or so he was throwing very hard. He was pleased to be throwing the ball reasonably close to the mitt that Carlos moved high, low, inside, outside and in the middle of the strike zone. He quit after a few minutes of real hard throwing.

"Too much wouldn't do me any good," he said. "Thanks a lot. Maybe we'll get a team practice tomorrow before we play Federal Friday. They could be tougher now than when they knocked me out in the first half of the season."

Carlos nodded. "A stock boy at the super market has a younger brother playing with Federal. He boasted that they are set to knock us off good." The smaller boy took off the mitt and regarded his puffed hand. "Tomorrow, I'll show him this hand. I'll tell him how tough Dinner will be when you pitch against Federal!"

Rain did not come down in such quantity Thursday; the sun came out in mid-afternoon. But Khoury Park remained quite wet. No practice.

It seemed that Friday copied Thursday in reverse. The sun shone all day, but rain sounded on the dugout roof just as Coach Walt Smith faced his team for the pre-game talk.

"In case we do not get this game in," the coach said, "I don't want you to get away without reminding you that Saturday is Khoury League fund-raising day at Broward Mall. We have been assigned the Mall Supermarket, The Butcher Boy shop and Mall Drugs. We will have four boys at each place, and if all of you can come, we can have relief boys for each station. Is there anyone who can't be at Broward Mall from ten to twelve o'clock Saturday morning?"

Nobody indicated they could not be there.

"Fine," Smith said. "Be in full uniform, except that you will be more comfortable wearing sneakers or regular shoes rather than baseball shoes. I'll see you all at the Mall Main Entrance a few minutes before ten."

A metallic voice blared from the public address horns. "In view of advice from the weather bureau that the probability of continuing rain for the evening is ninety percent, all games scheduled tonight are postponed."

The sun shone, the sky was cloudless and practically all evidence of a rainy week was gone by mid-morning Saturday. Coach Walt Smith had news for his Dinner boys when he met them at the Mall entrance.

"League officials have inspected Khoury Park and determined that conditions will be fine for playing this afternoon. The game we should have played last night is now re-scheduled to be played today at three o'clock. Federal boys are out collecting the same as we are, so there will be no advantage for either team, rest-wise."

The coach gave assignments for four-boy teams to offer slotted containers to people who cared to donate. The one-time salt, coffee, cereal or whatever boxes had been covered over with white paper and KHOURY LEAGUE THANKS YOU lettered on one side.

"You represent all Khoury League people," Walt Smith reminded. "Be courteous, whether people respond with money in the slot or not."

Joe Mancin, Mike Ortega, Paul Orton and Forest Ennis were posted outside Mall Super Market. Joe and Mike were one team, Paul and Forest the other. They alternated offering their collection containers to people coming in and going out of the market. Joe and Mike were near the *Out* door when a rather plump woman with white hair and a pleasant manner smiled at Orton while he offered the box.

"Would you like to help our Khoury League, ma'am?" Orton asked.

"Why, of course!" she glanced at the DINNER lettering across his shirt front. "Why, you're on my husband's favorite team! He goes to Khoury League games regularly. But I don't have a speck of money until I cash his paycheck. You see me when I come out. Now, remember!"

This was not an uncommon occurrence. None of the boys particularly marked the white-haired woman in his mind. It happened to be Joe who approached her when she came from the market sometime later, followed by a young man pushing her well-laden shopping cart.

"Ma'am," Joe began, "would you like to—"

"Are you the boy who—no, you aren't. You are bigger." She peered intently at Joe. "But it seems as though I've seen you someplace before."

"Yes, ma'am. Probably I was at the other door when you went in. It doesn't matter which container you put money into, it all goes to the League."

"But each of you likes to have money dropped into your box, don't you?" The woman smiled, took a coin purse from her hand bag and dumped its contents into her hand. "Let's see: three quarters, four nickels and three dimes."

She walked to Orton and slipped a quarter into the slot of his container, put another in the one Ennis held, came back and gave a third quarter to Mike Ortega. She stood in front of Joe, again peering at him closely.

"I just know I have seen you and I don't mean this morning. You look so awfully familiar!"

"He'll look awfully *bad,*" the youth standing behind the shopping cart said, "after Federal gets through with him!" He grinned good naturedly at Joe. Then to the white-haired woman: "He's the kid who was on the television with Lefty Vroeg and Mr. Smith last night. That's probably where you saw him."

"Why, of course!" The elderly woman positively beamed at Joe, as though she had scored a personal triumph. "My husband called me from the kitchen to watch. You're the boy who promised to win the whole ball of wax for the Dinners!"

"No, ma'am! That is, yes, ma'am! I mean yes, ma'am I was on the sports show, but no, ma'am, I didn't promise to—"

"My husband thought it was really something to promise something like that!"

"Ma'am, I didn't!" Joe protested. Somehow it seemed important to make her understand, but he did not want to appear discourteous. "It was like this, ma'am: Lefty Vroeg saw that I was petrified and he made the promise, not me!"

"Right on TV." The woman nodded, went on as though Joe hadn't spoken. She took Joe's container and slid the dimes and nickels through the slot. "My husband would want you to have the extra coins—for promising to win the whole ball of wax for the Dinners!"

CHAPTER TEN

Federal Versus Dinner

MIKE ORTEGA and Joe Mancin warmed up for Dinner, but a few minutes before game time, Walt Smith called Joe aside.

"Mike is going to pitch," the coach said without preamble. "You're entitled to know why, after the impression you may have from what I said the other night. Believe me, I still think that you are going to help us tremendously, and I meant what I said about working you on the mound."

He stopped a moment, then shrugged and went on.

"While I was being frank about sometimes messing things up in dealing with youngsters, I could have added that while I keep in mind that you boys are young, I still believe percentage baseball works out in the long run even in Khoury League. Federal doesn't have a single batter who hits from the port side of the plate; it's playing percentage to pitch a righthander against them."

Joe nodded. He was not sure that he was not more relieved than disappointed. *I don't need to worry about winning the whole ball of wax today,* he thought, immediately realizing that the bit about bragging brought out at the super market had been on his mind more than he thought.

Mike Ortega started the game as though he was going to be a large factor in any "ball of wax" winning.

He struck out the lead-off batter, fooled the next Federal boy to come to the plate on a good change-up which he hit weakly back to the mound for an easy second out, then induced the third batter to go after a bad pitch and pop to Lon Alfo behind second base.

"You're going to be mighty tough today," Coach Smith said as he gave Ortega an approving slap on the seat of his pants. "All right, gang, let's get Mike a couple of runs! Start things rolling, Pete! A few solid hits right off will show this cocky youngster he's not as good as he thinks he is!"

The Federal pitcher was the lad who had needled Joe Mancin in the game that gave Federal the first half lead—and who had been so obnoxious at Broward Mall on Khoury League Day. He gave evidence right off that he was going to be hard on batters this day.

Pete Inglis took a called strike, a ball, another strike down the inside edge of the strike zone. Then Pete swung at a fast ball that was almost in the catcher's mitt before his bat got around, and missed.

Dave Hammer lifted a lazy fly to left for the second out; Harry Tessario went after a teasing pitch a little high and outside the strike zone and popped up to the first baseman.

Mike Ortega started the second inning with another strikeout and when the next batter bounced to José and was thrown out, it seemed as though the Dinner pitcher was pitching a carbon copy of the first inning. But the sixth boy to the plate for Federal met Ortega's first pitch squarely and hard.

The ball was a fuzzy white streak from bat to Mike Ortega. He threw his glove up more in reflex action than conscious effort to field the drive, deflected the ball an inch or so and slowed it some—which may have saved him from sustaining a fractured collarbone. His glove was knocked off, the ball slanted against the top of his left shoulder and looped like a hit fly—straight into the hands of Harry Tessario at first base.

Walt Smith hurried from the dugout and met Ortega before he reached the foul line. In the dugout the coach removed the boy's shirt and felt his shoulder carefully asking, "Does that hurt? There? Tell me if it hurts."

Ortega winced slightly once, then quickly said, "It's okay, Coach. I slowed it so the ball kind of skidded off. It might be a little tender, but it won't bother my pitching a bit!"

"You have a bruise that will be black-and-blue in no time," Smith said. "There could be damage that won't show. You won't pitch anymore today!"

"But, Coach! I don't pitch with my left shoulder!"

"Dizzy Dean did not pitch with his toe, either," the coach said. "Dean was a star pitcher for the St. Louis Cardinals—he is a member of the Baseball Hall of Fame, now—who pitched in the 1937 All Star Game. A line drive broke one of his toes. He came back too soon, favored the bad foot and his pitching style was altered. Bursitis developed in his pitching shoulder, which ruined his effectiveness and shortened his career. A doctor will decide when you can pitch again!"

Bill Smith took his stance at the plate; Joe Mancin stood at the dugout entrance, waiting to follow Smith. Joe's pulse leaped when Coach Walt Smith looked at him, then dropped when the coach motioned Forest Ennis and Paul Orton out to the bullpen.

The Dinner catcher worked a base on balls from the Federal pitcher. Coach Smith called Joe back to the dugout as he started for the plate.

"They may figure I'm telling you to sacrifice," Smith said, "and it's a temptation to do just that. Bluff a bunt, maybe you can get him in a hole. But hit away."

Joe had an odd impression that Coach was about to say something further. He seemed to bite back words when he closed his mouth abruptly.

Blame it, Joe thought, *things* WOULD *turn out that I have to bat, just when he might have sent me to loosen my arm. Coach can't help but remember the clobbering Ennis took before; he has to know that Orton would never last practically a whole game. He might have put me in there to— cut it out, Mancin! He wants right hand pitching against Federal.*

As the pitcher delivered, Joe shortened his grip on the bat and squared away in bunting stance. The ball came in high and inside. They had expected a bunt, all right. He repeated the bluff when the second pitch came and the umpire ruled it was ball two. Two-and-oh. The next one would be in there, probably a fast ball.

The pitch was in the strike zone, but it was a good change-up. Joe was fooled badly, poked weakly at the ball. Then he nearly went after the fourth pitch but checked his swing in time. The umpire's call vindicated Joe's judgement, the pitcher was in the three-and-one hole.

"Make it be in there, Joe!" Coach Smith yelled. "Make it be in there!"

Repeating advice to the batter after using his name was Walt Smith's signal for the batter to take the next pitch. Coach was changing his hit-away instruction, playing percentage that Joe would draw a base on balls.

The Federal ace foiled the percentage, fired a fast ball that split the plate belt-high and induced Joe to swing at a pitch high and a little wide. The catcher juggled the missed strike and no play was made on Bill Smith scooting to second base.

Walt Smith beckoned to Joe. "Things worked out the same as if I *had* told you to sacrifice," Smith said. "I wouldn't say I was glad to see you strike out, but I am glad you'll have a little time." He held Joe's eyes and made a small headshake. "I've been thinking that there is more percentage against throwing Ennis and Orton against this team than in the right-handed-hitters-ruin-southpaws theory. Warm up as much as you can, you're going in to pitch!"

Joe did not have much time in the bullpen. Tom Dancer hit a two-and-two pitch and grounded out. Fred Cook went for a high fast ball on another two-and-two count and struck out. Bill Smith did not get past second base.

Walt Smith caught Joe's range-finding pitches while his son took as much time as he could to fasten shin guards and adjust chest protector. The umpire allowed Joe only three more pitches after Bill took the mitt from his dad.

Joe was nervous, but after going to a two-and-nothing count, he settled down. His arm felt loose. He buzzed three pitches through the strike zone; the Federal boy did not offer at any of them and Joe registered his first strikeout.

Lon Alfo gobbled up a bounder hit by the second batter and another strikeout retired Federal.

Coach Smith nodded solemnly as Joe came to the dugout. "Seems that the old percentage is in for a beating," he said dryly. "Beautiful pitching!"

The Federal pitcher turned in as beautiful pitching as Joe had exhibited, sent three Dinner batters from the plate on strikeouts.

In the fourth inning, Joe pitched another strikeout, a pop-up to Jim Kubelik and a roller to shortstop. For Dinner in their half of the inning, Hammer and Tessario hit grounders to short for quick putouts. Bill Smith dueled the pitcher, fouled off three pitches after the count was full, then singled sharply through the box—but Joe Mancin again struck out. The Federal pitcher came off the mound and jeered at Joe.

"This'll be the blow-up inning for the big leaguer's pal! It'll be more like a wad of used bubble gum you win instead of any whole ball of wax!"

Joe actually had not thought about the inning coming up being the fifth. Carlos brought his glove from the dugout. "Just don't think about it, Joe," Carlos said.

"This is only the third inning I've pitched." Joe shrugged.

He struck out two batters; the third bounced straight into Harry Tessario's hands. But the Dinner fifth was no more productive than Federal's. Neither team put a runner on base in the sixth inning.

The Federal pitcher went out of his way to jab another low-toned barb at Joe. "This is it," he said. "This is your sign-off inning, Mancin!"

Joe tried hard to keep from thinking that this would be the fifth inning on the mound for him— his jinx inning. He pitched carefully to the lead-off batter. The count went to three-and-two. Then the Federal boy undercut a fast ball and popped it foul behind the plate.

It was not a hard chance, the ball was coming down well in front of the screen. Bill Smith located the pop-up, threw his mask to one side of the plate and took three steps toward where the ball was descending. Just before he was under the pop-up, Smith suddenly fell sprawling. The ball bounced off his mitt.

Joe's next pitch narrowly missed the plate and Federal had their first baserunner. Joe drew a deep breath. He tried to block from his mind any thought of a jinx.

CHAPTER ELEVEN

Fact, No Brag!

"MY FAULT!" Bill Smith carried the ball half-way to the mound before he tossed it to Joe. "There should be nobody on and one out! All my fault!"

Joe said nothing. He was going back in his mind to something Lefty Vroeg had said. . . . *Bad breaks, poor umpire calls, errors—the pitcher has to put any thought of such out of his mind and concentrate on battling the batter up at the plate now. . . .*

Bill Smith crouched behind the plate, called for a fast ball and held his mitt chest high to the Federal boy. Joe glanced at the runner on first base, then pitched from the shoulder. The ball smacked into the mitt. Strike one.

Another to the same spot—no swing, strike two. Bill Smith signed for Joe's change-up and held the mitt steady. The batter swung hard, so far out in front that he missed entirely. Strike three, one out.

The next batter quite evidently had watched Joe's strikeout pitches closely. He was ready as the first delivery to him bored toward the strike zone. But he swung a little over the ball and topped it a foot in front of the plate. The sphere spun and might have kicked off foul, but Bill Smith leaped forward and grabbed it. Then just as he threw, he almost fell flat again. His peg was over the head of Pete Inglis covering second and out of reach of Lon Alfo, backing up the shortstop.

The runner from first did not slow, sped right on to third. Dave Hammer retrieved the ball and threw to Inglis. The runner who had reached first on Smith's error did not try for second. But now runners were at first and third and only one out.

Bill Smith called time. He came to the mound head down, looked up at Joe then dropped his eyes. "You should be out of the inning," Smith wailed. He shook his head. "What can a guy say after booting two easy chances?"

"Nothing." Joe took the ball from his glove and chunked it back into the pocket. "Everybody boots one sometime."

"Chew me out!" Smith blinked rapidly. "Go on, gnaw on me—I'll feel less like bawling!"

Joe shook his head, repeated, "Everybody boots one sometime."

The big left-hander turned on everything he

had and struck out the next batter. The final out did not come by the strikeout route but the easy one-bouncer back to Joe served the purpose equally as well.

In the dugout, Dave Hammer asked Bill Smith, "What happened? Your bad knee buckle on you, or something?"

Joe Mancin was leading off the inning and swung a couple of bats in front of the dugout while waiting for the umpire to call, "Batter up." He heard Bill Smith grunt.

Then the catcher said, "Thanks for the offer of an alibi, but I don't have any bad knee. Nothing happened except that I just plain stumbled—one clumsy foot over the other, you could say!"

For the third time the Federal pitcher struck out Joe Mancin. The shortstop came in behind second base to make a fine grab of Tom Dancer's ground smash and pegged accurately to nip him at first base. Fred Cook ended the seventh by popping to the third baseman.

Bill Smith took Joe's range-finding tosses, pegged to second, then yelled, "Keep after 'em, Lefty! I'll try to keep my big feet under control!"

It was the first time the catcher had yelled anything at Joe that was at all complimentary. The southpaw wondered whether the catcher was trying to let him know things had changed.

Joe "kept at 'em." He struck out the rival pitcher leading off, got the second batter to go for a teasing two-and-two change-up and roll to Kubelik, then ended the top of the eighth with another strikeout.

He felt wonderful. It was an extra inning, because Midget League is a basic seven innings, but it was more than that. It was the sixth inning he had pitched. He was past the fifth inning barrier for the first time. What was it Lefty Vroeg said? Something about taking his lumps, but they wouldn't get him out of there because it was any certain inning. Well, he knew another lefty named Joe Mancin who wasn't going to be "out of there" because of any supposed-to-be-jinx-inning!

Bill Smith sat beside Joe in the dugout. Joe was sure then that the catcher wanted to—to—well, it was never easy for anyone to come right out and say he'd been wrong.

"You're looking better all the time on that old mound," Smith said after a little time. "You're really *pitching!*"

"It's a good thing I'm doing something!" Joe shook his head. "I'm sure not doing anything at the plate!"

"You'll get hold of one."

"I don't know." Again Joe shook his head. "Next time I'm up there, I'm going to bunt! If you get on base, watch for it!"

"Suppose I get lucky and rap one for an extra base?"

"I'll still bunt. It'd be better to move you up than to strike out again!"

Kubelik walked to start the Dinner eighth, then was forced out at second when Alfo grounded to shortstop. When Inglis drew a base-on-balls, it looked as though Joe Mancin might not get another time at bat. If Hammer or Tessario hit safely, Alfo COULD score and end the game. If at least one of them got on base, Bill Smith would be up—and he was hitting Federal's ace pitcher as though he owned him.

Hammer hit a grounder to third, forcing Alfo and was nearly doubled at first base. Tessario struck out. The Dinner threat ended.

Joe Mancin set Federal down in one-two-three order in the top of the ninth. While they waited for the Federal pitcher to complete the preliminary pitches, Bill Smith and Joe swung bats outside the dugout.

"Did you really mean that about bunting?" Smith asked.

"I meant it. This guy has the Indian sign on me today. You get on base and I'll dump the first good pitch he throws me—unless Coach signals different."

"He won't. Wouldn't be playing the percentage to use up your best hitter sacrificing. All I have to do is get on, and I'll be ready!"

Dinner's catcher and Federal's pitcher again

dueled and for the third time Bill Smith won. He timed a three-and-two fast ball perfectly and smashed a line drive between left and center field. He made second base standing up.

"Follow it in all the way!" Coach Walt Smith called when Joe took his stance. "Follow every pitch in all the way!"

Repeating advice without using the batter's name was Walt Smith's signal for him to hit away. Joe glanced toward Bill Smith; he nodded.

The first pitch was headed for the strike zone, a fast ball. Joe squared away, ran his left hand along the barrel of the bat and held it loosely. He guided the bat against the speeding ball. The sphere rolled slowly toward third, four feet inside the line.

Joe ran as hard as he could and was surprised not to hear the smack of ball into mitt as he crossed first base. Then he saw the first baseman chasing after the ball that rolled forty feet into foul ground. The third baseman had made a hurried, wide throw.

Bill Smith was across the plate before the for-lorn throw from the first baseman reached the catcher.

The game was over.

Dinner, 1; Federal, 0.

Boys poured from the dugout and surrounded Smith and Mancin, leaped and hugged each other.

Walt Smith slapped his son on the pants and Bill gave him a wide grin. The coach grabbed Joe Mancin's hand. Carlos Vardez had brought Joe's glove and stood clutching it, looking at the big southpaw as though he was a god.

"You shake a man's faith in percentage ball," the coach said. "A batter with your power should have hit away—so you catch everybody off balance with a perfectly placed bunt! Every batter you faced was supposed to have the right-handed-hitter-versus-left-handed-pitcher edge—and all you did was pitch a no hit ball game!"

Joe stared wide-eyed. What Coach said was incredible. He actually had given no thought to anything except getting batters out. A thing occurred to him. He said, "Well, Mike pitched two innings and —"

"But you pitched seven!" Carlos Vardez cried. "The two of you threw an extra-inning no-hitter, but you pitched what would have been a regular game no-hitter!"

"Just that," Walt Smith agreed.

Bill Smith looked at Joe and the big pitcher recognized there would be no more barbed needling from the catcher. Then Bill eyed Carlos, nodded and winked solemnly.

"Fact, no brag," Bill said.